LIKE THE COMMON COLD, THE ONLY CURE FOR A HELLISH DATE—IS A GOOD LAUGH

That terrific-looking guy who went to Oxford made sparkling conversation, all right—with the other voices in his head. Then there's the fellow who wanted you to do something to get him in the mood—read him nursery rhymes! These are just a few examples of the unbelievably wild dates others have experienced—and lived to tell their tales. So sit back and laugh, if you can, at someone else's expense. But remember, any day now it may be your turn to top these stories of bizarre, incredibly dumbfounding dates.

MORE DATES from HELL

KATHERINE ANN SAMON has written articles for *Newsweek, Allure, GQ, Mademoiselle, Travel & Leisure, Harper's Bazaar, Vogue, Working Woman, Seventeen, Glamour,* and other publications. Originally from Texas, she now lives and works in the dangerous date capital of the world— New York City. *Dates from Hell* was her first book.

MORE DATES FROM HELL

True Stories from Survivors

KATHERINE ANN SAMON

A PLUME BOOK

PLUME
Published by the Penguin Group
Penguin Books USA Inc., 375 Hudson Street,
New York, New York 10014, U.S.A.
Penguin Books Ltd, 27 Wrights Lane,
London W8 5TZ, England
Penguin Books Australia Ltd, Ringwood,
Victoria, Australia
Penguin Books Canada Ltd, 10 Alcorn Avenue,
Toronto, Ontario, Canada M4V 3B2
Penguin Books (N.Z.) Ltd, 182–190 Wairau Road,
Auckland 10, New Zealand

Penguin Books Ltd, Registered Offices:
Harmondsworth, Middlesex, England

First published by Plume, an imprint of Dutton Signet,
a division of Penguin Books USA Inc.

First Printing, February, 1995
10 9 8 7 6 5 4 3 2 1

 REGISTERED TRADEMARK—MARCA REGISTRADA

Library of Congress Cataloging-in-Publication Data

Samon, Katherine Ann.
   More dates from hell : true stories from survivors / Katherine Ann Samon.
p.   cm.
ISBN 0-452-27097-9
   1. Courtship—Humor. 2. Dating (Social customs)—Humor.
I   Title.
PN6231.C66S19   1995
818'.5402—dc20   94-27818
                                                                        CIP

Printed in the United States of America
Set in New Caledonia
Designed by Leonard Telesca

Once more, for Larry
and for everyone who put out the word
or was brave enough to share a date from hell

Contents

Introduction

You read the first book, now read the follow-up!

Why a Walk on the Wild Side Continues

Yes, they're all true! That's what every television and radio host, reporter, and reader wanted to know about the dates from hell in the first book.

And so are all the dates in this sequel. The stories were shared by men and women of all ages across the United States who were willing to confess these real-life nightmares—as long as their names, and sometimes other identifying details, were changed. You'll see why you can't blame them.

There's no shortage of dates from hell. During radio interviews, we'd take call-ins, and outrageous dates would pour in. There was the poor woman in New Jersey who, unbeknownst to her, was on a first date with a Mafia hit man who just had to do one quick drive-by, shooting up a rival, then they'd be off to dinner.

There was the story that, in true Southern California style, came in via a car phone. A young man was despised by his girlfriend's parents. After dating secretly, the girlfriend took him to a party her parents were having. The boyfriend leaned down to talk to her mother, who was seated, and pat her on the head, then walked off. What he didn't know was that his college ring had snagged the woman's hair, and when he walked away, he had pulled off her wig, which was dangling from his hand, revealing an almost bald head.

Storytelling is alive and well when a date from hell gets rolling. We're living in a fast society, and if you can't produce something entertaining to share—quickly—then we're on to the next person. Any one of these stories stops everyone in their tracks. There's a plot, there's a punch line, and mostly there's a pathetic heroine or hero we want to root for—because we've all been there.

And storytellers and listeners have a lot in common: a sense of humor and the gift of empathy—you have to be able to put yourself in someone else's shoes, and relate. A superiority complex does not fly here, because what might have been a sensible solution to these stories is usually absent: In the crazy world of dating, there's almost never any such thing as logic, and even if there were, there's rarely an opportunity to deliberate.

These dates from hell come from smart, empathetic, optimistic searches for love. If our main characters made one repeated mistake, if there's one nugget of wisdom we can learn about dating and avoiding a date from hell, it is this: Get out of the date the instant your instincts tell you there might be trouble. It can only get worse.

If you date long enough, a date from hell is bound to happen. The saving grace is that you end up with a story to tell, your badge of courage from the dating front. You survived—with a sense of humor. And in today's world, that's nothing to take lightly.

We go on dates, and we listen to dates from hell, because dating is, in the end, the pursuit of happiness and love. These are true tales from the battlefront of dating, and they're stories that say a lot about us. Even when the going gets tough in love, we keep on going, trying to make things right, trying to make even the most embarrassing or tormenting situation end on an upbeat note.

Sit back and listen to one hundred real-life sagas that these men and women were brave enough to endure, and intrepid enough to share.

Why were they willing? Because they think the stories are fun—at least, that's what they think now that the dates from hell are behind them.

1

* * * *

You're the Date from Hell

Your date is looking horrified, and it's because she or he is traumatized by *you*. What got into you, what were you thinking—what were you *doing*? This time, it's time to pity your date.

idway through dinner on our third date, Gayle told me that she liked old-fashioned men. That was me! I was an old-fashioned guy.

We were at a fairly fancy jazz bar in Boston, having a delicious dinner, listening to great singing and piano playing from a guy we'd both read about. We kept our conversation low, so as not to disturb the music.

We were side by side in one of those small semicircular booths when I noticed that Gayle wasn't listening to my conversation about trading stocks on the foreign exchange. She was smiling lazily at the piano player. To make matters worse, he was staring back at her with the same sexy little smile. I drew an imaginary line from his eyes to my date, and the trajectory couldn't have been clearer: he was eyeballing her cleavage.

I just about choked on my raw oyster and gave her a tap that was a little too harsh.

"Do you two know each other?" I asked, hoping she would get the hint, would stop staring back at the guy, and would maybe tie a napkin around her neck to hide some skin.

She gave me a little laugh and said, "Very funny. He's great, isn't he?"

Oh yeah, he was great, and he looked a little like Jeff Bridges in *The Fabulous Baker Boys*. Next thing I knew, Gayle would probably say, "I know this song!" and start slithering on top of his piano, making goo-goo eyes at him.

"I've heard better," I couldn't believe I heard myself saying.

"I love him," she said, smiling more broadly at the singer, who smiled wider, too.

Was she breathing harder, or was I listening harder?

"Aren't you going to eat your food?" I asked, trying to drag her attention away from the guy.

She hummed along, running her fingers through her long brown hair, and her green eyes were half shut. That dreamy look was too much for me.

I dropped my oyster shell on my plate and glared at the singer. I put my arm across Gayle's shoulders and dragged her right against my side.

The singer said, "This is for all the beautiful brunettes in the world," and Gayle purred, "How nice."

"Is he bothering you?" I asked, angry. All she had to say was yes, and I'd deck the guy.

"No!" she said. "I love his music. He's got a great voice."

At the end of the song, Gayle clapped hard and the singer nodded in her direction and murmured, "Thank you."

That did it.

"Hey, buddy. Put the moves on someone else's date."

Did I say that? Yeah, I said that. And I'd stand behind it. At least until he stood up and I could get a better look and decide if he was much bigger than I was.

Gayle was shocked.

"Relax," she said, stroking my arm. "Nothing's going on. Please. Calm down."

The singer said, "And this one is for all the men who are lucky enough to be here with the brunettes in the world," but he stared at Michelle's cleavage some more, and it was clear to me that he was toying with me. He was going to seduce my date right in front of my eyes and still sound innocent about it. This guy obviously made a practice out of hitting on women and humiliating their dates night after night. Only this time, he'd chosen the wrong brunette and the wrong brunette's date to mess with.

"Don't do me any favors," I bellowed, clutching the edge of the table. To my date I said, "We're going."

She panicked and said, "Please, what's wrong? Settle down."

I brought my hands to my chest and bellowed, "What am I? A fool? I know what's going on here. The guy's been staring a hole at your cleavage for a half hour. He's asking for it."

Two waiters in tuxedos appeared, and I jumped to my feet, wobbling the table. I didn't want to be at a disadvantage when the punches started to fly.

The guys stood on either side of the singer. I gulped. I didn't think I could take on three guys all at once—a frontal assault would leave me in pieces.

The two guys took the singer by the elbows, and the singer got to his feet at the same time that one of the guys pulled his piano bench out for him.

The singer put an arm out in front of him, testing the air, and slowly turned toward the back of the room. I felt the wind come out of my sail, and I wished I weren't still standing.

"Oh, sit down," Gayle said in disgust, throwing her napkin on the table. "He's blind."

When the manager asked me to leave, I nodded like a whipped puppy and did as Gayle told me: I took her home. When she was getting out of the car and said, "This isn't going to work," I was chivalrous enough to know that she meant to never call her again. Old-fashioned men know not to continue the pursuit when they've been given the brush-off on the same night they've humiliated themselves.

—Glenn, 26, trader, Boston

✳ ✳ ✳

Cigarette smoking didn't bother him. It had been a long time since I'd asked a first date if I could smoke, and tonight, after three glasses of wine, I wanted one, and he said he didn't mind.

I held my hand low, so the smoke wouldn't get in his face. We both crinkled our noses. There was an odd smell.

I glanced down, and saw that I had burned a hole right through the leg of his pants, a little above his cuff.

I hoped he wouldn't notice. He did.

"Oh, no!" he said, flicking the hole with his hands.

"I'm so sorry," I said, wanting to sink into a hole. "I'm really sorry. They're nice pants. Are they new?"

Looking pathetic, he nodded and said, "It's just a little hole. Don't worry about it. Really."

I apologized again, and he poured us each another glass of wine and said, "Let's put it behind us. It was a simple accident, so don't worry about it. Do you mind if I bum one of your cigarettes?"

I said, "I didn't know you smoked."

He said, "I don't. I quit two years ago, but I feel like it tonight."

Whether he realized it or not, it was obvious to me that he wanted a cigarette because he was rattled by the hole in his pants. When he took a closer look, he'd see that there were two holes.

He bummed about five more, then got up and returned with a fresh pack.

"It's my old brand," he said.

I said, "Gosh, I hope this night doesn't make you start smoking again."

He laughed and said, "It already has! You have a gorgeous smile."

He melted my heart.

Once he opened the pack, he searched for a matchbook. Feeling cozy, I lit a match for him. He put a cigarette in his mouth and leaned the tip to the flame. He stared into my eyes, and I stared back.

He yelled, "Ow!" and rubbed his nose, his eyes watering. "You burned my nose!" he said, and accidentally knocked his pack of cigarettes off the table.

I sat and wondered what I could say next other than apologize. He was bent over for longer than he needed to be.

I leaned over to see what was going on. He was examining the second hole in his pants.

—Michelle, 34, environmental therapist, San Diego

✳ ✳ ✳

Business management class was the biggest snooze. It was a huge lecture class, and what kept me attending diligently was this cute brunette who sat one row down and two seats to the left of me.

After months of sneaking peeks at each other, I asked her out, waiting for a rebuff.

Her name was Shannon. She said, "I was wondering when you'd get around to asking."

Shannon and I went out twice, and on the third date, we went back to her dorm room. One thing led to another, and we made love.

At two in the morning, when her roommate was expected, I left.

I took the long way back to my dorm, enjoying the night, thinking what a great girl Shannon was.

I was just about to turn up the sidewalk to my dorm when someone called my name.

It was an old friend, Chris, whom I'd gone to high school with. I hadn't seen him at all this semester.

We said hello, and I invited him up to my room for a beer.

My roommate was out of town, and Chris said, "I'm glad we're alone, and I'm glad I ran into you. I was just wandering around, and I need a shoulder to lean on. I don't have a friend at school I've known as long as you."

I hoped he wasn't going to make a confession about coming to terms with his sexuality or something. I was feeling too lighthearted to have a serious talk.

He said, "About fifteen minutes ago, my fiancée called and said she was calling off our engagement. She said something happened out of the blue. She'd had a date with some guy, and they'd gone to bed with each other, and she said he was so great, that there was no way she could go through with marrying me. How's that for my male ego? What am I going to do?"

Poor guy. Here I was, falling in love, and he was getting his heart snapped in two.

"What's her name?" I asked, draining my beer.

"Shannon," he said. "For one thing, I'm in love with her name. What am I going to do? I feel like hell."

This was a setup, I just knew it. It wasn't a coincidence that he was in front of my dorm. He was gunning for me. One false move and he'd come after me.

I said, "Who's the guy?"

Chris stood up. Unable to control himself, he burst into tears and said, "I don't know! She won't tell me. But when I find out who he is, I'm going to kill him, then hire some people to beat him up for me every week. What would you do if you were me? I feel like the world just caved in."

Well, it caved in on me. I'd busted up my friend's engagement. But he'd get over it eventually.

Of course, Chris was the state wrestling champ in high school, and you didn't want to provoke him.

I knew I wasn't going to stop seeing Shannon, though. The bottom line was, I'd have to keep a real, *real* low profile.

The worst part was that Chris poured his heart out until four in the morning, telling me what a great friend I was, that he hoped we'd be friends for life, making me feel guiltier and guiltier.

—Ted, 20, student, Austin

❋ ❋ ❋

Mac, my compadre, said he was going to get a date for me. He went out with a different girl every night of the week, and I didn't think I'd had a date in three years.

Last night, at a bar we all hang out at, Mac said, "Hey, Bobby. I got you a name and phone number here. You just have to call her."

I did. Two nights later, I told Mac, "I got me a date Saturday night with that girl you told me to call!"

Mac said, "All right! We'll all be here waiting for you Saturday night. Bring her by."

Saturday night, I went to the bar, and my friends all shouted hello to me. Mac said, "Where's the date?"

I said, "Ah, *hell.* I *knew* I forgot something. I was working on my car engine all day, and I must have just plain forgot about her."

Mac said, "Now we know why you don't have dates."

Right about then, the bartender hollered, "Car on fire!"

Mac and I raced to the parking lot. There was my car, up in flames. I must have wired it wrong when I was working on it.

Mac said, "You ain't got no woman. And now you ain't got no car."

—Bobby, 22, construction worker, Atlanta

❋ ❋ ❋

Cameron arrived at my doorstep in a black double-breasted blazer, a starched white button-down shirt, pressed khakis, and shiny brown penny loafers. He looked mainstream.

I was wearing one of my favorite outfits: long flowery dress, black combat boots, and I had pulled up my hair into a bun that I had secured with two wooden chopsticks—and, because it was a date, our first date, I had pulled on silver bracelets that went halfway up my forearm.

We looked at each other, and it couldn't have been more obvious that we marched to a different drummer.

We both said something like, "Nice outfit ...," and I grabbed my tapestry backpack and we went out to his four-door gray Ford Tempo.

"Is this a company car?" I asked, feeling proud of my observational skills.

"No," he said. "Why?"

Another nice job of sticking my foot in my mouth, I thought, shriveling with mortification.

He stared at me, turned on the ignition, nodded to my boots, and said, "Tank division?"

I felt my cheeks burn, then I saw that he had a small smile on his face, and decided he had a loose side after all. The date might not be a total loss.

We drove to my favorite macrobiotic restaurant, which he said he was willing to try if I didn't make him eat a bowl of seaweed, but it was jammed. Because we were both starving, we agreed to a pizza parlor that we were coming up on.

We made an odd entrance, anyway, so overdressed, and so differently, that people stared, but we joked about it.

We were seated in a booth alongside a table of goons who stared at us and made private jokes. Consequently, our conversation froze after ordering a large mushroom pizza, salads, and jumbo diet sodas. To break the ice, I told him a joke.

The joke was only a five on the joke meter, but, I suppose because he was tense and a little nervous, he laughed too hard.

He leaned his head back and laughed even louder, which embarrassed me, so his laughter wasn't contagious. People at tables around us were gawking.

Cameron was still guffawing when he leaned forward to give in to another round of belly laughs. When he lifted his head to laugh some more, our eyes met and we realized at the same time that he had leaned so far forward that his right nostril had locked around his soda straw. He looked like a walrus with the straw sticking out of his nose. He stopped laughing, and I started.

He reached up to take it out, and accidentally shoved the straw further up his nose. Cameron looked horrified, and I was still laughing. He turned his head to the right, as if he was trying to shake it loose, and the straw banged against the top of the Parmesan cheese dispenser, and little drops of blood appeared at the edge of his nose.

I fell sideways on my side of the booth, laughing like a lunatic. The more traumatized he looked, the harder I laughed. The more I tried not to laugh, the more I did. I looked up to see Cameron cross his eyes, like Pinocchio, to get a better look at the straw, and I laughed even harder.

Cameron rallied and yanked the straw out, but I was in the middle of one of those hysterical laughs that wouldn't stop.

Cameron canceled our order and drove me home in silence. I asked if we should go to the emergency room, and I broke out laughing again. The horrible thing was, I liked him.

—Kristy, 18, graphic artist, Philadelphia

* * *

Panhandling was paying off in a nice way. I'd never done it before, and once I got the swing of it, profits were coming in, even if they were coming in one coin at a time.

The reason I was out there was that I didn't have enough money for dinner.

I'd taken my date to a Greek restaurant in Greenwich Village. I was nuts about her. She was a Winona Ryder look-alike, an ace student in our English class at Columbia University, and it was our second date.

All through dinner our waiter had been drooling over her, asking if her food was good enough, giving her extra glasses of wine on the house, batting his long black eyelashes at her long black eyelashes.

Serving our coffee and dessert, he started singing softly in Greek to the background music, staring at my date, then put his hand over his heart and backed away. My date thought he was charming. I thought he was a jerk who needed to button at least one button on his white shirt and take off one of his five gold necklaces—maybe the one with the big round gold medallion that hung past his pectorals.

The bill came, and I realized I had zero money. I didn't have a charge card, and had forgotten my bank card.

I didn't want to ask my date for money, so I said, "I have to go to a cash machine. You stay and finish your coffee and I'll be right back. Wait here."

I walked a block away, used my last fifty cents for a coffee to go that I gulped, and set up business on a corner, holding out my empty paper cup.

"Bail me out!" I yelled to passersby. "My date's inside, and I ran out of money! Help! I love her!" The money trickled in, fifty cents here, a quarter there. At that rate, I'd be there all night.

A homeless man stood beside me, smoking a cigarette butt. I thought he was going to fight me for the corner. Instead, he said, "Not bad. *I'm* convinced," and watched from a few doors down.

"My date's stranded in a restaurant! I don't have enough money! She'll never go out with me again! Help me out for love!"

I got a lot of smiles and "Good luck!"s, and I got two dollars from a mom, and two dollars from a businessman—those were my biggest donations. I sat on a stoop and counted. $5.73. It was a respectable amount, but not enough. I'd have to go back to the restaurant and ask my date for money, or call a friend to come give me some.

I was walking back to the restaurant when my date came running down the sidewalk toward me. She was glowing and smiling.

"Great news!" she said, breathless. "I couldn't wait, I'm so excited! Dinner was free! Can you believe it?"

She threw her arms around my neck, and I took them off me.

"What? How?" I wasn't relieved at all. Something was fishy.

She was practically bouncing on the balls of her feet.

"When you were gone so long, the waiter said he'd make a deal with me. If I gave him a kiss, he'd tear up the check! That's all! One kiss!"

I felt my temper wake up.

"How much of a kiss?" I asked.

"How much? I don't know. A little one. Very small."

"On the lips?" I asked, starting to breathe hard.

"Uh, yeah. Real quickly, though. No big deal."

"Any tongue action? Any at all? Did he try? *Did* he?"

She stared at me and said, "No. Chill out."

I stormed to the restaurant, throwing open the door like it was at a saloon and marched up to the waiter.

I pointed my index finger and wagged it right under the waiter's throat.

"Hey, buddy! Yeah, you! I'm talking to you! Look at me when I'm talking to you! She's my girl! She's *my* girl!"

The waiter acted like I was a gnat on an elephant's rump, looking right past me, which just made me madder.

"You don't kiss my girl! Hey! You know what you are? You're a coward! Yeah! You don't kiss my girl! She's my girl *and* she's my date!"

The waiter wearily said, "Congratulations. Excuse me while I take this wine to table three."

"Hey!" I yelled, following him, pushing around a table and getting back in his face, shaking my finger under his nose again. "How'd my girlfriend pay you, anyway? Huh? *Huh?*"

The waiter said, "We worked it out."

That made me even more furious.

"You pig!" I yelled. "You know what you are? Why'd you do it, man? Why'd you do it? That's all you did is kiss her once, right? Don't lie to me! Don't lie to me!" Now I was getting carried away. I think I was getting into character, and I liked it. It was fun. I was wild, like a Ferrari on an open road.

"Don't lie to me, man!" I yelled again.

Two waiters materialized, and each one grabbed one of my elbows. One of them said, "It's all right, guy. It's all right. Settle down."

I twisted in their grasps and said, "He kissed my girl! He kissed my girl! I have my dignity!"

The waiters conferred, and one said to me, "That's true. Sit down and stay still. Don't move."

I did as told, my adrenalin pumping so hard that my legs were shaking. My date stood by the door, looking horrified.

The kissing waiter appeared, flanked by the other two, looked to the side, and said, "Accept my apology."

I was ready to lunge for his throat, but I was tired, and it was getting late.

I said, "Okay."

One of the elbow-holding waiters handed me a five-dollar bill and said, "Your date left this on the table by accident. Take it, and go."

I stood up, shrugging my shoulders around in my jacket like I'd seen tough guys do in movies, and snapped the money out of his hand, saying, "Thanks. I will."

On the street, I said, "Wow! Can you believe that? What a night!" I started shadowboxing. "Here's enough for coffee somewhere and I'll still have money left for the subway! Plus,

I have money in my pocket that I panhandled tonight! We're rich!" I shadowboxed again, and said, "What a night!"

My date stopped, crossed her arms over her chest, and said, "Are you out of your mind or something? That was wild."

I put my arms around her thighs and lifted and spun her around. I felt mighty. I sat her down and waited for her to say, "You were wonderful back there!" She didn't. She glared at me.

I thought she'd be thrilled that I'd been willing to fight for her honor.

"Everything was great till you picked that fight," she said.

We walked twenty blocks before she'd talk to me, and then it was just to tell me what a jerk I was. I still felt pretty good, though.

Even so, I took a deep breath and said, "Accept my apology, please."

She shrugged, considering it.

I held out the five dollars to her and said, "You didn't really leave this on the table. It was a bribe from them to get me out of there, and I'm using it as a bribe to get me back in your good graces. Maybe you'll take it and buy me a donut and some coffee?"

She snapped it out of my hand and said, "I will. I'm too tired to argue. Just don't do that again."

I wanted to shadowbox some more, but I was afraid she'd deck me.

—Jacob, 18, student, New York City

✳ ✳ ✳

I was a film critic for a neighborhood newspaper, which meant that I went to at least five movies a week. I took friends with me a lot, and on weekend nights I took my date if I had one. I liked the feedback.

I was out with a woman I'd been trying to get a date with

for two months, but our schedules never meshed, till tonight. We were at *The Piano* with Holly Hunter.

She was shooting me piercing looks, and finally whispered, "It's a pet peeve, but I hate it when someone rumbles in their popcorn bucket for ten seconds, then takes out one kernel. I can't hear the movie!"

"Well," I said, "Hunter is a mute in this movie, so relax."

That was pretty witty, I thought. I was near the bottom of the barrel, so I set it on the floor.

She was touchy, but everyone had a quirk you had to overlook.

"Great scene!" I said. "Did you see that camera angle? Wasn't that great?"

She whispered, "Sh. Didn't you hear everyone 'sh' you? Whisper."

I rolled my eyes. No one had sh'ed me.

Fifteen minutes later she whispered, "Can you stop squirming? You're making my chair bounce."

I said, "Enjoy the movie. *That* was a *great* line! Did you hear Keitel's line?"

She swiveled away from me.

I said, "Want me to get us some more popcorn?"

A man in front of me said, "If you don't be quiet and stop eating and opening candy wrappers, I'm going to kill you."

I said, "Okay, okay. Sorry."

To my date I said, "What a Type A."

The guy whipped around to give me a hard stare, and my date got up and went to the ladies' room, not coming back.

When the movie was over, I found her in the lobby.

She said, "I think we have a problem here. You go to the movies all the time, so that's a big part of your life. And I have to be honest, you and I have completely different styles of movie-watching. I like to sit quietly and talk and eat when the movie is over. This isn't going to work out. Let's not prolong it. You're a great guy, thanks for the movie, but I have to go. My nerves are shot."

I watched her go, another Type A. They were all over the place.

—Derek, 41, film critic, Dallas

✳   ✳   ✳

Johnny was so great-looking that every major fashion designer in the world was using him for their fashion shows and advertising. He was tall, had dark hair and huge brown eyes, and, of course, was in great shape. He was a few years younger than I was, mild-mannered, and had a sensitive side to him—no swagger or bragging.

We met at a party, and he started dropping by my office to have lunch. I had several other gay men friends, so I wasn't a bit uncomfortable that Johnny and I were becoming fast friends. He was nice, and fun, and I liked going to the movies or shopping with him. It was great having a new friend who was so easygoing. I could completely be myself with Johnny, and not have to put on a "dating" personality.

After dinner at my apartment one night, I started complaining about my neck, and how I was going to have to schedule a massage. Johnny said, "I could give you a massage sometime."

Being the massage junkie that I was, I immediately said, "Okay!" and jumped onto the floor, sitting cross-legged.

Johnny was a good masseur, and I was completely relaxed, so I wasn't sure whether, after a while, he was kissing my neck or just had incredible fingers. No, he was kissing my neck!

I jumped to my feet, horrified, and said, "*What* are you doing, Johnny? You're gay!"

I wasn't sure I wanted to be the one who changed his sexual preference, nor was I interested in him sexually. After all, I'd come to see him as a younger brother.

Johnny, still kneeling, said, "I'm not gay. Whatever gave you that idea? I *like* girls. I like *you*."

Huh?

I said, "But you're gay!"

Johnny, looking shocked and confused, said, "No, I'm not. I've never been. I don't like men. I like *girls*. I like *you*."

Me? Sexually? Johnny was straight? Uh-oh. It was an understatement to say that I felt bad. I was embarrassed, but he looked mortified and beyond hurt.

After a few seconds, I got myself together and tried to make light of the situation by joking, "Well, now that I know you're straight, you can start paying for everything!"

I expected a laugh, but Johnny sincerely said, "That's not a problem," and he broke my heart. Oh, no. He was still being nice. Maybe if he'd gotten mad, I'd have felt a little better.

Well, we talked about nothing important, and, fortunately, he left after a few minutes.

I felt horrible that I had hurt him so much. Now that I thought about it, I couldn't remember what had made me think he was gay.

Johnny and I went out a few more times, but the friendship faded out.

He had everything going for him, but I wasn't interested in him romantically. Granted, I thought of him as a little brother. But we had also gone past the early stage in a friendship when there was the possibility of romance.

But if *I* was embarrassed that I had read him wrong, I could only guess how *he* felt about it.

—Paula, 23, art gallery assistant, New York City

* * *

Brooke lived in Los Angeles, I lived in San Francisco. We'd met at a wedding. She was a friend of the bride, I was a friend of the groom.

My first visit to see her, I asked her to pick a restaurant.

We sat down, opened our menus, and I said, "*Uh*-oh. This is really pricey. I can't believe these prices."

Brooke said, "Should we go? No? Okay then, what will you have?"

I said, "I'm looking for an entree under twenty-five dollars. Give me some time."

When the waiter appeared, Brooke said, "I'll have the shrimp with cilantro pesto to start, and—"

"That's twenty dollars!" I said.

"—and the grilled salmon."

I did the price check on aisle three, finding grilled salmon, and said, "Thirty-seven dollars for a piece of salmon? Well, I guess I'll have the hamburger. That's all. And more bread. No wine. Can you bring us some water?"

Brooke waited until he left to say, "You asked me to make reservations at a nice restaurant. You specified a place that had at least two stars. I think we should cancel our order and leave."

I said, "No, no. Waiter! I'm changing my order. I'm having . . . the . . . grilled vegetables, and the lamb chops. Cancel the burger. And, a bottle of wine."

That was a fast fifty-eight dollars. But to Brooke I said, "I feel much better now that I did that! Tell me some more about your job."

I ate fast, which made her start eating fast. I wanted to get out of there. I couldn't believe when she asked if we should order dessert and coffee. The fact that she asked told me that she wanted it, so we did.

When I got the check, I said, "One-hundred-seventy-five dollars and thirty-three cents? What is this? Someone's car payment? Tickets for two to Jamaica? This is outrageous!" I took out my credit-card-size calculator and began tallying. I called the waiter over. "That bottle of wine was thirty dollars, not thirty-five. Did my regular coffee really cost as much as her decaf espresso? What's the deal? Are you charging for refills? Can I see a menu again? I just want to look over a few things, if you don't mind."

Brooke said, "I can't bear this. I'll wait for you outside."

I said, "Go ahead. Do you want twenty dollars to tip the coat check woman? How about another twenty for the valet? If you stand in one place for too long, they'll charge you for that, too, so keep moving. One-hundred-seventy-five dollars and thirty-three cents. . . . I could eat for a month on that. . . . This is not a happy meal, that's for sure . . ."

—Jim, 32, computer salesman, Los Angeles

✳ ✳ ✳

Nervous? Was he kidding? I was petrified.

It was only our second date, for crying out loud, and there I was in his mother's drawing room. Who had drawing rooms anymore, for heaven's sake? Bryan's mother was dressed like the Queen Mother, and I was wearing dungarees, a T-shirt, and sneakers. And she was having tea poured for us by a maid.

"*Yes,*" I whispered back. "Totally. Let's go."

Bryan patted my knee, said, "Mother, I'm going for a quick walk. That'll give you two some time to get to know each other without me hovering."

So then it was just the two of us. She was sitting on the edge of her seat, her back as straight as a board, her chin precisely parallel to the floor. If she were my teacher, I'd know I was in for trouble.

Fidgeting, I asked, "Do you mind if I smoke?"

"Not at all," she said.

A maid produced an ashtray and matches for me, then disappeared. I lit up, concentrating on not dropping ashes on the Persian rug.

"Tell me," said the Queen Mother. "How exactly did you and Bryan meet?"

That was a good one. We met at a bar. We were drinking tequila shots, and we hit it off.

"Through mutual friends," I improvised. "You have a great house. When was it built?"

While she told me, I smelled something odd. So did she. She wrinkled her nose a few times, sniffing the air. I sniffed, too.

The maid entered, whispered in the Queen Mother's ear, and calmly escorted her away. To me, the maid whispered, "Fire!"

I looked behind me. Fire!

I tended to wave my arms a lot when I talked, especially when I was nervous. My cigarette must have seared the floor-to-ceiling damask curtains behind me, because now they were on fire.

I helped the maid get the fire extinguisher going, and we put out the fire before it crawled across the curtain rod. Then I waited outside on the front porch steps.

When I saw Bryan on the sidewalk, the first thing I said was, "Suppose I was facing your mother, and there was some strange activity going on behind me. Would your mother notice?"

"Of course not," said Bryan. "She hasn't had her cataract surgery yet. Why? Was there a problem? What's that smell?"

—Sarah, 27, bank teller, Cleveland

* * *

Timing was the key.

We were at a lecture by a woman who was supposed to be an authority on the Impressionist era of art. I didn't know two cents about art, but my date, Claudia, loved it. Claudia reminded me of Audrey Hepburn, with the same graceful beauty and softness. She was the most cultured woman I'd ever been out with. Hey, I went to college, got a business degree, but I skipped all those fruity art classes, and lately I got most of my culture from David Letterman's show. So I talked a friend's uncle at the museum into getting me two tickets. Claudia had been impressed, murmuring, "The lecture is sold out. You're incredible."

That night, at the lecture, I was feeling pretty incredible—yeah, I scored big on this gig. It was a yawn for me, but Claudia was rapturous, hanging on to the speaker's every word. I looked like I was absorbing it. Every now and then the audience burst into loud applause as the speaker first made her case for some artists' rights of expression thing, and I applauded wildly, too.

About fifteen minutes into the talk, my stomach felt funny, like it was getting bloated. It was nothing, so I distracted myself by thinking that Claudia and I were going to make a good match after all. If she'd go to a sports event with me for every arty thing I went to with her, we might have a real good thing going.

Uh-oh. My stomach was gurgling and when I put my hand on it, it was puffed, and tight as a drum. I looked to both sides, but the place was crowded; everyone's folding chair was pushed close together and formed semicircular rows, and I couldn't even see a way to exit to the men's room without making a major disturbance of myself. All I could do was keep my stomach muscles tight.

The plan struck like lightning. I'd wait for the next huge burst of applause, and if I needed to relieve my little bit of gas, that would be the time—no one would notice, and my discomfort would be over.

The key was perfect timing. Right then the speaker was making little points, and I decided to wait until there had been a couple of rounds of lukewarm applause—that would mean a burst of clapping frenzy on the next emphatic point the speaker made. That had been the pattern of applause.

There were the two rounds of moderate applause. It was coming up—the big windup. There was the pitch: The speaker burst into, "Creative minds cannot be corralled by banal bureaucratic bluster!"

I slammed my hands together to applaud and let my stomach muscles relax. All I heard was my one crashing clap, and the mighty volume of escaping gas that sounded to my flaming ears like the noontime whistle at a factory.

No one else had clapped. I was the only one.

I closed my eyes, wanting to die, then opened them quickly, calling on childhood protective devices to guide me through this humiliation: I sat still, a small, serene, I'm-lost-in-thought-about-this-great-lecture smile on my face, and hoped someone near me had the look of guilt. I had no shame—if someone else became the scapegoat, fine with me. I prayed that no one was pointing my direction behind my back. So far, I believed, I had not been pinpointed.

However, I heard one or two people nearby cough. I saw another person tilt away. I heard some snickers. But mostly, out of the corner of my eye, I saw Claudia ever so slightly lower her face into her Hermés neck scarf, until it covered her mouth and nose.

The speaker had stopped talking, searching the back of the room for the disturbance; then she continued. I waited for the next blessed burst of applause, then, hunched over, excused my way to the back of the room, and waited for Claudia outside.

We made small talk on the drive to her house. I was driving fast, but she didn't comment. She had her hand on the doorknob before I pulled to a complete stop. She waved good night and walked quickly to her door, and I zipped off, thankful to rid myself of any vestige of that horrible moment, knowing I wouldn't be going out with her again.

Shortly thereafter, when I applied to medical school, I had to explain to the interviewer why I expressed a preference for one particular specialty of medicine.

"Why gastroenterology?" the interviewer inquired, ready for a well-rehearsed save-the-world answer.

Well, that was the kind of answer I gave him, even though I knew the real reason: Claudia.

—Elliot, 25, gastroenterologist, Washington, D.C.

✳ ✳ ✳

K eeping myself in check had been my mission. The guy I was going out with, Sam, was a gentle soul. He was a social worker, and active in his church. Out of his big bunch of brothers and sisters and his crowd of friends, he was the official leader. In short, he was levelheaded, rational, and wise beyond his years.

I guess I was a little more spontaneous than he was.

We were at an outdoor cafe with a group of his friends from work, and the margaritas had gone straight to my head. Tequila always made me active, and I was feeling rambunctious. I was also getting miffed. The waitress, wearing her little halter top and short shorts, skimming by us on her roller blades, was giving Sam the eye. When she stopped by our table, she stared into his eyes and leaned over as much as she could and as long as she could. On her third stop-by, she finally got Sam's full attention. His eyes were glued to her, and they smiled at each other.

When she stopped by the fourth time, I slurped the remains of my third margarita and said, "Don't you have a bra you can wear or something?"

Everyone at our table stopped talking. The waitress put her hands on her hips, leaned back, looked at Sam, and said, "Can I get anyone anything else? Like maybe some coffee for your friend?"

I glared at her and said, "Bring me another drink, if you can do it without blowing a blade."

The waitress said, "Say, honey, what's your problem?"

That did it. For some reason, something snapped. As I got

to my feet, I threw my water in her face, then banged the empty glass on the table.

She sputtered and shook her head to get the water out of her eyes, and I said, "I'll take that coffee now."

Sam gaped at the waitress and said, "Just the check." He looked at me and murmured, "You're sitting next to my boss." Then he pulled out my chair, drove me home, and didn't even say goodbye.

—Amy, 19, yoga instructor, New Orleans

✳   ✳   ✳

She said, "Sure! I'd love that!"

I was disgusted. I said, "Why don't you just say no if you want to. I can tell that you don't want to go out again. You're good-looking, and I'm not. You don't mean it."

She looked mortified and said, "No, really. I'd like to go out again."

"But just as friends, right?" I asked, sneering. "I doubt I'll ever get to even kiss your cheek. You're just feeling guilty. Why lie?"

She gulped and said, "Don't be so hard on yourself. I'm sure there'll be someone for you one day. We just didn't click, that's all. You're not so bad-looking." She was holding her purse to her chest, gauging the distance to the door of the restaurant.

"Oh, sure," I scoffed. "Like I don't know I'm hard to look at, what with this acne and the scars from my car accident. Why lie?"

She stared at me, and said, "It's not your looks. I guess, if you don't want me to lie, it's that you're kind of hostile. I'm just being honest." She stood and added, "I'll call myself a taxi."

I said, "Leave. You think I'm not good enough for you? This is a brush-off, isn't it? Why lie?"

She went into a phone booth, shutting the door, and when her call was finished, she stayed in the booth, pretending to read the phone book, but keeping one eye on me.

After ten minutes, she ran for the door where a taxi had pulled up.

I let two days go by, then I called her at the office.

"Hi, it's me," I said. "Say, you feel like going to Jamaica with me for two weeks? Why not? I'm not good-looking enough, right? Why lie?"

—Zeke, 38, salesman, Detroit

* * *

2

✷ ✷ ✷ ✷

Exploding Endings

There's the finish line! You almost made it! This is one date that's going to end well—isn't it? Then, suddenly—*ka-boom!*

We'd made it to the good-night kiss without a hitch.

My date, Tim, owned a sporting goods store and was a fanatical athlete. While we kissed, I could feel the muscles in his back.

At first the kiss was so passionate that it made me swoon, but then, as it continued, my mouth began to hurt. Tim was really throwing himself into things, obviously trying like crazy to be the most amorous kisser ever. Instead, I was thinking that he was the most athletic kisser.

Keeping his lips latched to mine, Tim had taken my head between both his hands. I felt like I was trapped inside a football helmet.

I tried to twist my head away, but Tim, who was concentrating, held fast, working away on my lips until I felt a twinge and then heard a pop.

He leaned back, and I pulled my head back and said, "Ow! That hurt! You know what? You kissed me so hard that it was like having my lips sucked up by a vacuum cleaner. You either broke something in my lips or suctioned something out of *joint* in my lips."

He smiled and said, "I kiss like I do sports. I don't hold back. Your lips are fine."

I said, "No, they are not." I felt my lips and said, "See? They're swelling."

Tim's eyes opened wide as saucers and he said, "Oh, no. They're getting huge."

We stepped into my apartment and he closed the door behind us.

"What should we do?" he asked, looking stricken.

I tried to bring my hand to my lips, but two flotation devices directly under my nose got in my way. They were swelling like mad now, and hurting, too.

"Kuh nuh-nuh-nuh," I said, walking toward a mirror and gasping at my Donald Duck beak.

"What?" he asked.

I had said, "Call nine-one-one," but nixed that idea and looked at the clock. Ten-thirty. I dialed my doctor and repeated the incident three times before he said, "Oh! *Oh!* That's interesting. Sounds like he popped blood vessels in your lips, particularly in your upper lip. Ice it, and see me in the morning. And stop kissing him."

I made Tim drive me to the emergency room anyway, but when we got there, I couldn't bring myself to go in and explain things. I told him to circle the block, and when I still couldn't get up the nerve to go in, I said, "Tuh muh huh," which meant, "Take me home." I had to say it three times, working up to the top of my lungs.

At my house he started to open his door to help me down the sidewalk, and I shook my head at him. He leaned forward, absentmindedly going for a kiss, but I pushed him away. He didn't have any trouble with my parting words: "Suh luh."

So long.

—Casey, 23, diction coach, Cincinnati

❋ ❋ ❋

Walter was a manager at a bank, and was the godfather to a colleague's two daughters. He sounded like a good blind date, and he was—until we went back to my place around midnight for a nightcap.

I collect stuffed animals—bears, specifically—from all over the world. My family traveled a lot when I was a kid, and so my collection was extensive and precious to me. I had built a shelf about eighteen inches from the ceiling where I displayed them. The shelf ran down the entry hall and across two walls of the living room. Two magazines had even photographed my collection over the years.

Walter said, "Never seen anything like that. Can you take down a few?"

I took them down one at a time, telling him a brief sentence or two about each bear. I guess I got carried away, because when I stopped, I had taken down about fifteen.

He had lined them up on the sofa, which was touching. He had a gentle side, and I liked that.

Walter leaned down to inspect my favorite, and smacked it in the face with his fist. I was stunned. He used a left hook on the next one, then picked up the third and pummeled it with his fist.

I rushed over and said, "Stop that! What are you doing?" The bear's face was smashed in.

Walter said, "They're not real! Look at my lips. *They're not real!* They're toys! I'm just goofing around. Give me that one. I'm not through."

He yanked it out of my hand and started punching it again.

I got it away from him, and he reached for my bear from Switzerland, poking it in the muzzle with a fork he grabbed off the counter.

I yelled, "Stop it! Stop it right now! You're upsetting me!"

Walter torpedoed the bear into the arm of a chair, straightened his suit, and said, "What are you gonna do? Call the fuzz? Get it? Fuzz? Cops? Fuzzy bears? Chill out. Is there any more wine?"

I should have kicked him out right then, but I was in shock. I had never seen anyone, even under the age of five, behave like that.

He made some small talk, drained his glass, then snatched up a baby bear and stuffed its muzzle into the wine glass, its little eyes hanging over the sides of the glass in alarm.

I stood up and said, "Good night."

He said, "Good night to you, too," and went down the row on the couch, belting each bear in the tummy.

"I'll call you next week!" he said in the doorway, trying to get a kiss, but I kept moving my face. "And I'll take a rain check on that kiss. Bye, kids! See ya next week!" and he threw some imaginary punches before I slammed the door in his face.

—Penny, 32, kindergarten teacher, Maryland

✳   ✳   ✳

Tahiti was paradise. Back when I was twenty-seven, I was the skipper of a pleasure boat and had made Tahiti my base. To top it off, I'd had my third date with the most beautiful, sweetest woman I'd ever met. She was Tahitian, so I was going to be careful about courting her just right.

This was our fourth date. I had picked her up very early on Sunday morning, before the tourists woke up, to go to my favorite big market. We practically had the market to ourselves. We picked up a gorgeous fish, vegetables, fruits, and huge bouquets of flowers. We had the first choice of the very best of everything. We got back in my jeep and were heading to my place, where I was going to prepare for her the best lunch I knew.

It was a heavenly day to be driving along—clear sky, balmy breezes, a beautiful, quiet, soft Sunday morning.

All of a sudden, I felt harpooned. My groin felt like it was in flames. I slammed on my brakes, stunned. What had happened? It hit me again—blinding, hot pain. Had the wind flipped an ash from my cigarette onto my pants, where it burned through, setting me on fire?

I bailed out of the jeep, beating my pants with my hands. Yikes! There it was again, an agonizing, searing sensation.

Without hesitating, I shucked off my pants and sat in the middle of the road, examining my thighs and lower legs. There it was again, misery, at the hem of my underpants.

Out the corner of my eye, I saw the jeep start to roll. I tried to get to my feet, but the pain jerked me back to the pavement. I saw my date hop out of the jeep, managing to grab only a bouquet of flowers.

I noticed something else, too. I heard little titters and soft laughs. I saw a ring of white shoes, the hems of freshly starched gingham dresses and men's dress pants.

I had the double misfortune of stopping my jeep in front of the little Catholic church, which had just let out. The Catholic Tahitians had all witnessed my disrobing and genitalia inspection. Tahitians, who love laughter, had stayed to watch.

They all gave a collective "Ooh!" when a red, three-inch centipede crawled out of my underpants and across the pavement. Then I heard the second, more subdued "Ooh . . ." when we all saw the stricken look on my date's face before she started walking home.

—Reed, 55, retired, Delaware

✳ ✳ ✳

Now they had their heads together, tittering behind their menus about whether or not Hank and I were hitting it off.

Needless to say, I was on a blind date. I was on the worst possible kind—where the friends who set it up were not only wildly in love with each other, they were hoping that their two friends would fall in love, too.

I didn't think there was a chance of that.

Before tonight, when I'd asked my friend to describe Hank, she'd said, "He has a *great* voice. And he looks really good in hats."

Huh? In pants, or hats?

"*Hats,*" my friend had said, as if sharing some sexy secret with me.

Well, that was incentive enough to get me to go on that blind date.

Hank was nice, but not as dynamic as he'd sounded on the phone, and he wasn't wearing a hat, which was a letdown.

As for me, I'd been bright and perky on the phone because my friend had told Hank that I was always like that. However, that was an exaggeration. Tonight, so that I wouldn't let Hank down, I was so bouncy and peppy that I almost made myself sick. I could tell from one of Hank's split-second looks of boredom that I wasn't his ideal dream date, either.

But the night wasn't a complete loss. We had a nice big booth in a cute pub. Our dinner was just fine, except when our friends would start giggling behind their menus and ask, "How are you two doing?"

When Hank and I would turn to each other and one of us would say, "Let's kill them," our friends would erupt into gales of laughter, but we would be dead serious.

Hank asked the waitress for our check, and I let my breath out. That was one of the longest dinners I'd ever had. Finally this night was coming to an end. I had been smiling so much that my face ached.

Suddenly, in the back of the restaurant, a chorus of "Happy

Birthday" rang out. A flock of singing waiters and waitresses was heading our way, and Hank and I craned our heads behind us to see who the embarrassed recipient would be.

That would be: Hank and me.

The singing bunch stopped right in front of us and started their song from the top, belting it out this time, and the words stood out. They were singing, "Happy Blind Date to You!" and they were singing directly and loudly to Hank and me.

Our friends were pointing at us and laughing so hard that they were crying, falling all over each other on their side of the booth.

Suddenly all the drunks in the pub gathered around our table and joined in the third round of "Happy Blind Date!" as the cake was placed in front of us.

Hank and I couldn't look at each other. My friend was laughing and crying so hard that she got out of our booth and pushed her way to the back of the pub. Clearly, this great idea belonged to her and her boyfriend.

Hank and I blew out the candle so the crowd could applaud and make lewd comments.

My girlfriend's date said to us, "How about *that*? What'd you two think? I'll bet you were surprised! You were surprised, weren't you? How's that for putting the cap on a blind date? We thought that up, by the way." Hank and I just nodded, not saying anything that expressed our gratitude or envy of this originality.

Hank and I tossed some cash onto the table, and we got up. Guys in the crowd were slapping Hank on the back, saying, "Go get it, man! You can do it! We're behind you!"

To me, some girl said, "You got that look of luv, honey!"

Some other guys gyrated their hips wildly and let loose with what seemed to me to be pig-related calls.

We burst through the door, relishing our freedom from inspection. A few minutes later, our friends joined us, still laughing and humming "Happy Blind Date."

We smiled lamely, waved goodbye, and I followed Hank to his car.

At least we had conversation for the ride to my apartment, and it consisted of how much we hated our so-called friends.

Even with all that in common, we never went out again. And I'll kill anyone who ever has any rendition of "Happy Birthday" sung to me in any restaurant, any time.

—Joanie, 23, reporter, Idaho

* * *

New Year's Eve was usually fifty-fifty: Either it was a great night or a total bust, but nothing in between. My date for this New Year's Eve was a guy, Drake, I'd been dating for a month. I liked him, but we were stalled in the romance department. Rather, he was stalled.

His kisses were always quick, chaste, closed-lipped. When I'd push for more, he never budged. He was a pretty good kisser, but there was just so long I could keep my lips pressed immobile against someone else's before my mind started to wander to grocery lists and stockings I had to wash out. I was not going to let this one detail be enough of a reason to dump him, however.

The party was deluxe, and we were dressed to the nines. He had on a tuxedo, and I was in a long, dark blue strapless. I wore my hair up, and had on the diamond and gold earrings that I'd inherited from my grandmother.

It was almost midnight, and Drake was loosening up more than I'd ever seen him. He was drinking the champagne like it was water.

He had just given me one of his pursed-lip kisses, but then—what a shock—he gave me a real, passionate kiss. Then he started smooching me on the neck, and then around my right ear. I was so surprised that I didn't stop him, just monitored his progress. He was nibbling my ear too hard, and I shrugged as a hint to ease up a little. He switched to the left side of my neck, and chewed on that ear for a second or two. At the stroke of midnight, he gave me a huge kiss, then nibbled both my ears some more and practically gnawed on my neck.

He excused himself, and I took out my compact, thinking that even though Drake's behavior was a vast improvement, he needed to be reined in a little.

I took a closer look in the mirror. My earrings—my *pierced* earrings were gone. They were completely gone, posts and all. He'd chewed them right off my earlobes, and then swallowed them whole.

Helping a guy get through his awkward kissing stage was one thing, allowing myself to be a grazing ground for a jewelry eater was quite another. This guy would need too much tutoring in the art of love, even for me. At 12:10 A.M., I knew this romance was history.

—Louise, 20, hairdresser, Montana

✳ ✳ ✳

When I was in my early twenties, I was trying to impress a woman who was at the International Institute for Education with me. She was cultured, worldly, and beautiful.

It was the early forties in New York, and I'd discovered a drink at the swank San Remo bar and restaurant in Greenwich Village. The drink was "Café Reale," which was an espresso with a shot of anisette, and it was fabulous—I thought it was the greatest drink in the world.

I took her to a French bistro for a long, terrific dinner, then walked to the San Remo to have a Café Reale for the perfect cap on the evening.

As she drank hers, I waited for her comments of appreciation. She drank some more. No comment.

I was annoyed. How could she not comment on this masterpiece of a beverage?

To prompt her, I said "It's unusual coffee, don't you think?" She shrugged.

I said, "Don't you like it? I love it."

She said, "You must realize. I'm Armenian. This is what we drink whenever we think we're catching a cold."

That was the end of my savoir-faire.

—Arthur, 78, architect, New York City

✷ ✷ ✷

Summer meant being able to spend more time at my beach house, which I had just finished renovating in Galveston. I was going to take a week of my vacation at the house, and invited a new boyfriend, Patrick, to join me.

We'd been out together three other times, so I felt comfortable with him, even if we hadn't slept together yet. I had a hunch that this would be the week that we crossed that bridge, but I gave him his own bedroom anyway.

The first day he was charming, repeating that he'd fallen in love with the house. That night, he turned in early, explaining that he was exhausted.

The next morning he was chatty, said he wanted to take a walk on the beach, and didn't return until dusk. Once again, he turned in a few hours after dinner.

On the third day, at breakfast, I asked, "Is there something wrong? Anything you want to talk about? You've been distant with me."

He put down his glass of juice and said, "I'm glad you asked. Now we can get this out in the open. Basically, you're not young enough, beautiful enough, or thin enough."

Stunned, I said, "For what?"

He said, "For me."

I felt like I'd just fallen overboard. I heard him add, "But you're a fabulous friend, and I love being here with you. Why don't we keep things platonic?"

A platonic relationship didn't bother me. What bothered me was suddenly feeling old, unattractive, and overweight—as if my one desirable asset was my house.

I said, "Why not? Because that'll be impossible when we don't have contact with each other anymore. Pack your bags and leave immediately."

He actually cocked an eyebrow, looked at me solicitously, and said, "Are you sure you want that?"

—Harriet, 45, film editor, Galveston, Texas

✳   ✳   ✳

Cristal was not a champagne I ever saw in the bargain bin. But there I was, sharing a bottle of it with Karl on our second date.

We had met while sitting in the reception area of an accounting office on April 15th. His opening line had been "So, we're both procrastinators." It was true. What had become true later was that we were at opposite ends of the stratosphere where income—among other things—was concerned.

We had been at the nightclub for five hours, dancing, talking, and drinking. It was a crowded Saturday night, and Karl had used his VIP status to get us past the waiting mob. At two in the morning, I was ready to go home.

Karl said, "No problem. I'll call a car." He worked on Wall Street and used the company's car service to get home to Connecticut every night.

In the car he pulled me close, and I rested my head on his shoulder, telling him what a great time I'd had. It was the truth. I really liked him. He was sweet, and a gentleman.

After a few blocks, he said, "I'm staying at a hotel tonight. Why don't you join me?"

I laughed and said, "Thanks, but I don't think so. We just started going out."

He said, "Okay. I'll stay with you at your place."

I laughed again and said, "Very funny. Let's not rush things. Besides, we have a date to see each other Monday night. That's only two nights away. I'll see you then."

He said, "I don't think so." He pushed me away from him, looked at me intently, and said, "Driver, stop the car. Take her to her apartment, then wait for me at the club." To me he said, "If you won't sleep with me, I'll go back to the club and find someone else who will. In case you missed my drift, you won't be seeing me Monday night or any other time."

He got out of the car and slammed the door.

The car hummed, going nowhere. I was stunned. What had happened to my gentleman?

I gave my address to the driver again, as humiliated as I was mad and proud of myself for not giving in.

I felt better, though, when the driver said, "That guy was a real putz. You feel okay?"

I was starting to.

—Sandra, 24, paralegal, New York City

* * *

Wealth wasn't even on my list of what I wanted in a man. I had a more realistic set of criteria. But the fact that my date that night was wealthy beyond belief, with well-invested old family money, sure didn't hurt.

We met at the health club—one of the most exclusive in Chicago. We'd been stealing glances at each other for a while when I was on the Stairmaster and he was on the rowing machine.

Even so, I was startled when, one night after work, he came over to the machine I was working out on and started talking to me, suggesting that we have dinner together after our workouts.

I didn't believe in playing games, putting off a date if I were free, so I accepted, grateful that I always lugged around a well-stocked workout bag.

We got in a cab and headed to a restaurant he knew about.

Once inside the café, he chose a table by the bar. We had drinks, nibbled on peanuts, then took advantage of the Happy Hour buffet of miniature pizzas, mini hot dogs, and meatballs.

When the staff started to clear away the buffet, my date leapt to his feet, returning to the table with a mountain of treats heaped on a plate.

An hour later, having devoured the free food, I wasn't hungry, but I did want a salad or something else healthy.

"Let's check on our table," I said.

My date said, "I didn't ask for a table. Happy Hour food is always good enough for me. Say, do you mind if I smoke? Great. Can I borrow three singles from you? I know for a fact that the machine only accepts one-dollar bills, and all my bills are bigger."

Simple, understandable request. I handed over three dollars.

He came back to the table, smoking, and said, "This went well, didn't it? I'd better be going, though. I've got a busy day tomorrow. Waitress! Check, please."

He set a platinum charge card on top of the bill, which was about twenty-three dollars with tip. The waitress said, "Sorry, sir. We don't take that card."

He rifled through his wallet and said, "That's the only one I brought with me."

The waitress said she'd take a personal check.

My date dipped into the inside breast pocket of his suit jacket and said, "I don't have it with me."

The waitress, clearly frustrated now, said, "We always take cash."

My date opened his wallet, looked at me, and said, "I can't

believe this. I only have two fives. I must have forgotten to go to the cash machine."

Having been in his shoes before, I sympathized and said, "Don't worry. I'll get this," and I paid the bill. Besides, there was something endearing about a moneybags being unable to pay a small check. It was sort of sweet and brought out a small nurturing side in me.

Once outside, my date said, "Shall we share a taxi?"

In the taxi, I gave the driver my address, then told him that he'd be making a second stop at my date's home.

When we got to my apartment, I said, "Thanks. That was fun. I'll see you at the gym tomorrow night, I guess."

He nodded. I waited. No kiss? I opened my door slowly, giving him an opportunity to delay me. He grabbed my hand nearest him and squeezed.

I smiled. I knew what was coming.

He pointed at the meter. It read four dollars.

I said, "What?"

My date said, "Oh, pardon me. I was under the impression that we were sharing the taxi. My fault. Sorry."

I sank back on the seat, shaking my head. What a cheapskate. How much worse could it get?

I owed him two dollars, plus fifty cents for a tip. Having given him my singles for his cigarettes, the smallest bill in my wallet was a five-dollar bill.

I held up the five-dollar bill and said, "This is all I have," expecting him to say, "That's okay, I'll get this."

I was about to tuck the bill back inside my wallet when he whipped it out of my hand and said, "That'll do. Good night."

—Betty, 22, secretary, Chicago

✳   ✳   ✳

Having just transferred from an all-boys boarding school, I was lost when I started public school my senior year. Everyone else seemed advanced on the subject of dating, and considering that it was 1969, they were all cool and into hippie clothes. Cool and hippie were two elements that definitely weren't let in the front gates of my old prep school.

I wanted to ask out Dierdre, but I knew she was way out of my league. She was supercool, and a certified hippie, wearing beads, flowing dresses, and buckets of patchouli oil. We had typing class together and she was nice to me, so I asked her out, waiting to get shot down. She looked me over, and I could tell she was thinking of turning me down, but she accepted.

Trying to be as hip as someone who wasn't could possibly be, I consulted an older friend and came up with my dating plan.

I took her to see Frank Zappa's movie *200 Motels*. It was very strange, which I decided was cool and would make points with her. It did. I'd made it! We'd had a very good date.

On the drive back, I ran out of conversation.

After a lull, she said, "Santana. Are you into it?"

I said, "No. Who's Santana, anyway?"

She was shocked. "Who *is* he? My brother and I are in a band, and Santana is the *only* music we play. The only music. Where have you been? Drive faster. I want to be home as soon as possible."

And that was that. Twenty years later, I produced a two-hour documentary on Santana. When he asked me why I was interested in him, I said, "Well, you blew a date for me. That made me listen to your music, and I've been hooked ever since."

—Nicholas, 40, radio producer, Philadelphia

✳ ✳ ✳

Five weeks into our relationship, my feet still hadn't touched ground. Vincent was successful, attractive, smart, and highly romantic. Two weeks ago, he'd surprised me with plane tickets to the Caribbean for a long weekend. He had flowers delivered to my office every week. And he always secured the corner table at the most romantic little restaurants in town.

We were having a picnic in the park—his idea—and were finishing off the last of the wine. Vincent had brought pâté, cheeses, breads, cherries, and a small container of caviar. It was the end of another wonderful date. Afterward, we packed up and strolled along, swinging his big, antique picnic basket between us, giving each other kisses.

"Let's do it," Vincent said, giving me another kiss in front of a reflecting pond. "Let's make a wish."

We put the basket down beside the pond, and I felt my heart swell. I was in love with a crazy romantic.

"I don't have any change," I said, holding out my arms.

Vincent gave me a debonair grin, said, "Never fear," and reached in his pocket. He held his palm out to me.

"You go first," he said. "I hope we're making the same wish."

Normally, a comment like that would make me ill, but I knew what he was referring to—that would probably be the night we slept together.

How much should I toss in? I reached into the pile of coins in his hand, going for a penny, and pulled out a ring. A man's ring.

I held it up to my eyes. "Carol and Vincent, married November 1994." Married? A few months ago?

He looked chagrined, shrugging his arms and clenching his teeth. That was his total reaction.

I was deflated. All that was left to do was consider the kind of goodbye. I could toss the ring into the pond, saying, "I wish you sheer misery," but instead I held the ring out to him and didn't say a thing. He wasn't worth a fight or tears.

Funny thing is, I was sure I put the ring right in the center of his hand, but he fumbled it, and the ring plopped into the water. It seemed appropriate. When I left, he had rolled up his shirt sleeve and was trolling the scummy bottom of the pond with his wedding-ring hand.

—Judy, 30, engineer, Maine

✳ ✳ ✳

At least there was something to look forward to.

My blind date with Tray had been going well in a lukewarm sort of way, nothing great, nothing bad.

Over dinner we covered the obvious information quickly. He was a writer, and seemed as bored with his work as I was with mine, so I talked about everything *but* work.

Maybe because we were stumbling for conversation, we got onto the subject of relationships—even though it was our first date. He said he'd mostly had a string of blind dates.

Tray continued, "But I always have really good blind dates. I know how to do this. I get a lot of information on the person beforehand—I ask the person who's setting us up to tell me all about her. Then I have a lot to ask and talk about."

I said, "So, you must have a lot of mini-relationships, right? I mean, if the blind dates go well, they lead to second and third dates."

Tray said, "Not always," then got me to talk about my last boyfriend.

At the end of the night, he was walking me home, and the topic of blind dates came up again.

I said, "You're really fixated on that subject, aren't you?"

He said, "I ought to be. I'm writing a book about it right now. Each date is going in the book."

I said, "Even me?"

He yawned and said, "Yup. Well, I had a great time."

"I guess I won't be seeing you anymore," I said.

He asked why, and I said, "I wouldn't be a blind date any-more, and that's the only kind of date you go out on, isn't it?"

He laughed and said, "Don't read into things!"

Naturally, I never heard from him again. If I wanted to know what he thought of our date, I guess I would've had to read the book.

—Anna, 35, assistant chef, Florida

＊ ＊ ＊

For a few years in the eighties, Nell's was the hottest club in New York City. It had cozy, overstuffed furniture, and attracted the biggest celebrities. I only had one Nell's experience.

My blind date of the month, Jeremy, chose to meet me at a hip restaurant in Chelsea, which scored big points with me. The place was a cross between a bistro and a diner. He was waiting for me at nine, as planned, at the bar, wearing all black, with his blond hair slicked back. He looked great. I had one moment of wondering if I measured up, but he gave me a good once-over and a big smile and said, "You're the best-looking blind date I've ever had." Mutual admiration on appearances never hurt when you were holding your breath about a blind date.

Jeremy turned out to be more than skin deep, as well. He was a painter who had just moved from Michigan, and there were a few galleries already interested in his work. He seemed genuinely drawn to the fact that I was a photographer who shot interiors for catalogs.

After dinner, he said, "Usually I'd end a blind date right here—don't want to risk the ruin of a good thing, you know. If it works out well, I like to take things slowly. But this was the best date I've had in ages. So-o-o, do you feel like staying out later? Making the date last longer? We could maybe go to Nell's?"

Considering that the feeling was mutual, and I'd been hearing about the club, I agreed.

As we walked there, Jeremy held my hand and kept smiling at me while we talked. Standing at a crosswalk, I turned to tell him something and he gave me a terrific kiss. "Next time," he said, "you have to plan the evening."

There'd be a next time? We were already in agreement on that? Great.

When we got to the club, the throng had assembled at the red velvet rope and spilled into the street. A guy in front of us ground out a cigarette on the sidewalk and said, "I've been waiting two hours. You'll never get in."

Jeremy kicked over an empty produce box that was near the curb and said, "See if you can get a better look."

I stepped up on the box, and he put his hands on my waist to steady me.

"I've got an idea," I said, surveying the crowd, and jumping off the box. "They have a little path they've cleared on the sidewalk for pedestrians. Let's walk through like we're on our way somewhere else, and then stop and look and blend into the front of the crowd."

Jeremy took my hand and we casually walked in front of Nell's and paused at the red rope.

Like a miracle, the beefy doorman pointed and said, "You, you, you, you and you, wait over here." Jeremy and I were two of the people he'd signaled!

We did as he said, and Jeremy whispered, "Don't look so excited. Act nonchalant. Tell me about your apartment."

I mumbled a few fractured descriptions; my concentration was on the entrance to the club. I was so close—let us in!

After twenty minutes, the doorman said, "Okay. You two and you two."

He had pointed at us first! I took off for the door like a rocket, Jeremy right beside me. The red rope lunged in front of my waist, cutting me off from Jeremy. The giant crossed his arms and shook his head at me.

"You said I could go in!" I cried.

Jeremy, his face twisted in rage, stormed back from the entrance and said, "What's going on here? She's with me! You have to let her through. You pointed to her."

The giant shook his head.

"No," he said slowly to Jeremy, barely above a whisper. "I pointed to you and the other three."

"You can't split up a couple!" Jeremy said, irate. The giant was impassive.

I wanted to fall into a crack in the earth. My date had been selected, and so had a man and two women behind me, but not me. I lacked the "cool" quotient.

Jeremy reached over the rope for my hand.

He said, "What a jackass! This is an outrage! This is *absurd*! I can't believe this!"

I nodded, seeing his outrage, waiting for him to take his sword and slice the rope in half, and whisk me into the club with him.

"You should be getting in with me!" he continued, obviously fuming. "But since you're not, let's not lose our heads."

I pushed through my humiliation to focus on his lips and the words they were forming.

Jeremy continued, "We waited long enough, and the goal was to see what the inside looks like, right? And you and I are a team. So I'll go in and look around real fast, and come back out and we'll go somewhere else and I'll tell you what I saw. What do you say? No reason for this part of our night together to be a total bust, right? Give me five minutes. I'll be right back."

He was gone in a flash, leaving me to face the giant.

I waited forty-five minutes. I actually thought he'd be back.

Sunday afternoon, Jeremy left a message on my answering machine. As his message was coming in, I was thinking, *What a jerk. Good riddance.*

"Hi-i-i... it's Jeremy, around ... three o'clock.... I have a killer hangover.... The club was great.... I have tons of stuff

to tell you. . . . Call me—but not now. I'm going back to sleep.
Call me around eight. . . . You'd love the club. I'm sure I can
get you in next time. . . . Bye."

Really?

—Peggy, 27, photographer, New York City

* * *

3

✴ ✴ ✴ ✴

Tics & Quirks

Bizarre, idiosyncratic, peculiar. There's only one other word, hopefully, for the odd habits and behaviors some dates have: unique.

Frank had attended Oxford, was part of the group of twenty-something bright stars "on the hill"—in politics in Washington, D.C. He had a Great Dane and two cats that all adored each other. His small apartment was filling with carefully collected fifties furniture he picked up at flea markets and refinished himself. He played squash three times a week, and worked on a twenty-year-old Saab that he kept in top shape. He took me to hear a local band on our first date, then we went backstage to meet his friends in the group. He was smart, steady, handsome, sensitive—and hip. I thought he hung the moon.

Our second date was going well. We started by meeting at Kramer's, a great bookstore where there was a little cafe in back. We had browsed through the stacks, and he'd bought me *Like Water for Chocolate*, telling me how much he loved the romance of it, and how much he wanted me to have my own copy. We were only a few blocks from my apartment, so I asked him back for a drink. Neither of us felt like late-night barhopping.

He was sitting in the living room, inscribing the book for me, while I fixed us both a scotch and water. I leaned over to put his drink on the coffee table, and he leaned forward, too, and said, "There's something I want to ask you. It's kind of personal."

I took the book from him and read, "To a woman who's beautiful, smart, and sensitive, just like this book. Love, Frank." Whoa. My cheeks felt hot. That was flattering. What more could I ask for?

I sat on the floor, on the opposite side of the coffee table, took a gulp of my drink, and said, "That's so sweet. I think you're great, too, you know. What'd you want to ask?"

The question, I was sure, was, "Are you seeing other guys?" to which I'd say I wasn't, and the night would only get even more wonderful.

He leaned forward some more and said, "Do you ever hear voices?"

"Pardon me?" I asked, feeling my heart sink.

"Do you ever hear people talking to you inside your head, that only you can hear? Telling you things? Like this morning. I was sitting at the counter at a diner, and when the waitress served me, one of the voices said, 'That's not your toast. You ordered whole wheat, not rye.' "

He was staring at me intently, motioning with his hands that he was waiting for my response.

"Well," I said weakly. "Was the voice right?"

He gave me a large nod.

"Yeah, it was. I *had* ordered whole wheat."

"Huh," I said, racking my brain for something to say. Finally I came up with, "That's great. At least your voices are right about things."

I figured the best approach was to act nonplussed, like this was a regular conversation for me, nothing out of the usual.

"What do yours say?" he asked.

"Well, I haven't thought about it. When I can think of an example, I'll let you know. Are you through with your drink? Let me take your glass. It's getting late."

"Do you think it's odd that I hear them?" he asked. "Granted, they mostly dispense solid advice."

"No," I said, wiping the coffee table, signaling that it was time for him to go. "Not at all. Why?"

"Well, I used to have a roommate. And before he moved out, he told me that I should seek professional help. It occurred to me that he was covering up, you know, that he had his own voices and didn't want to admit it, so I've been keeping tabs on him, you know, following him sometimes, to see where he goes."

"Hm," I said, wondering if it was time to panic. "I see your point. You're probably right." I yawned and said, "Wow, I'm bushed. Well, this has been a fun night."

Fortunately, he got to his feet and said, "Yeah, it was! I'll call you later in the week. Let me know how you enjoy the book. Do you read Spanish? One of my voices does. I can lend you the untranslated version, if you like."

"Great!" I said, holding the front door wide open, overriding the impulse to say that I didn't, which would only prolong his stay. However, it did occur to me that, aside from Spanish, I knew he spoke French and Italian. Hearing a few voices now and then wasn't such a big thing, was it? Maybe it was just intuition, or instinct on his part. He probably wasn't a complete oddball. I'd give him another chance if he asked me out again.

We gave each other a kiss, and he murmured, *"Hasta la vista,"* and I closed the door.

Those voices were giving him ace instructions on kissing. I hoped he'd call tomorrow.

From the hall, I heard, "Yeah, it definitely looks like rain. No, go ahead. After you."

I looked through the peephole in the door, wondering which of my neighbors he was getting in the elevator with. I hoped it wasn't the nosy guy down the hall.

There was only one person in the elevator—my date.

"Lobby?" he asked loudly, pressing a button and staring straight ahead, which meant he was staring right at the peephole.

I pulled my head back.

As the elevator doors were closing, I heard him say, "I'd love to!"

At least his voices were still dating him, because I wasn't anymore.

—Gina, 19, model, Washington, D.C.

* * *

S usie had worked with my brother two years earlier. My brother ran into her at a drugstore, they started talking, and he said that he had a younger brother she might want to meet. She'd given him her number, and he'd passed it to me, saying, "Stop spending your weekends at my place. My wife thinks you're a side table. Call this girl. She's nice and she's pretty."

Susie invited me over for dinner, and when she opened the door, I grinned. She actually was pretty.

When I stepped in, I sniffed the air.

She took my jacket and said, "I wondered if you'd notice! I have five cats, and my neighbors say that they can smell the kitty litter box all the way in the hall, but you couldn't, could you?"

I thought for second.

I sat on the sofa and accepted a beer. I leaned back and crossed my leg, and jumped. An odd furry creature was on the outside of my thigh!

I brushed it away, but it stuck to my hand. I looked closer. It was a huge fur ball.

She said, "Oh! That's from the dogs. I had a dog walker take them out for a spin so I could finish getting dinner ready."

I sat down again, handing off the fur ball, and said, "So you and my brother worked at the same photocopying store a few years back?"

Three cats marched through the room, leapt onto the couch, and lined themselves up on the back of the sofa, forming an odd sort of neck pillow for me. One put its paw on my head.

"Cute cat," I said. "What kind of dogs do you have?"

"They're mutts, from the same litter. A brother and his sister. I think there's some sheepdog in them, and some Bernese mountain dog, and some shepherd."

The huge dogs came in and leapt on me, and my pants were covered in fur. Following my instincts, I touched the back of the sofa and saw that it had an inch-thick coating of cat and dog fur.

Before I could help myself, I said, "You need a maid."

She smiled and said, "You probably do, too. Don't be embarrassed. I hear it all the time from my friends. They won't come over here anymore, can you believe that?"

She said she'd ordered a pizza, and apologized for not cooking.

I said, "I love pizza. I don't care if you cook or not."

The pizza arrived, and she griped that it was ice cold, and said she'd reheat it.

I smelled something vaguely charcoal-y and sniffed around her kitchen, opening the oven.

"Geez!" I said, using a dishrag to reach into the oven. "You're supposed to take the pizza out of the box! It's burning!"

She said, "Huh. That's odd. I do it all the time and it doesn't burst into flames that often."

I didn't know what to say that wouldn't hurt her feelings, so I nodded and said I was going to the bathroom to wash my hands.

In her bathroom, I gagged, pulling my shirt over my

mouth. That wasn't a kitty litter box, that was a toxic-waste dump.

I turned to leave the room when I saw a box radio plugged into the wall and perched on top of the horizontal rack above the tub. A blow-dryer was slung over the rack beside the radio, and also plugged in.

I unplugged them both and took them to the kitchen with me.

"Do you know that you're going to kill yourself with this radio arrangement?" I said, gasping for semifresh air.

She squinted and said, "You're a real worrywart, aren't you?"

I said, "Why's the hair dryer plugged in and hanging over your tub?"

"Oh! The only plug in the bathroom is high up and near the tub, so that's why. That's as far as the wires will reach."

"That's horrible. See this warning tag on the dryer?"

She laughed and said, "I don't have water in the tub when I dry my hair, you nut! The tub is always drained!"

I wiped my forehead and saw that I had a big, furry paw for a hand.

A few minutes later, I pushed aside some cat hairs from my side of her cluttered dining table, took a bite of pizza, and pulled a tuft of cat hairs out of my mouth.

I took a sip of soda, straining for the hair with my front teeth.

I finished that one piece and couldn't get any further. Two cats had jumped onto the table, curling up between our plates, and a third jumped onto the table, landing right on the pizza.

She picked the cat up, dropped it on the floor, and took another piece for herself.

I watched the clock and realized that my nose had gotten used to the situation. I pulled a long white hair out of my mouth and watched as the dogs leaned against my legs, sleeping. They were so big that I thought their weight might break the front bones in my legs.

I struggled to free my feet, and stood up. In the mirror, I could see that the entire back of my body, from head to toe, was covered in a long blanket of cat and dog hair.

My date had stopped looking pretty about forty minutes ago.

I stretched, watching hairs float off my arms, and said, "I better get going. I had a busy week."

She said, "It's so early! Why don't you stick around and we'll watch TV?"

I didn't answer, but I did take my plate to the kitchen. There, in one electrical outlet, was a flimsy adapter into which she'd plugged a toaster, a portable oven, a blender, and an answering machine. Into the side of the adapter she'd plugged another adapter that serviced a food processor, a coffee bean grinder, and an electric skillet. There was so much stuff that the counter was completely covered.

I said, "There's a fire in the making here! You can't have all this stuff plugged in like this! It's dangerous!"

It was also disgusting. Everything was wrapped in hairs.

She said, "You know what? I think you *should* go. You're acting like my father or something. I've gotten along fine without you, you know. I know how to handle the circuit breaker, and the fire extinguisher is right here and I know for a fact that it works perfectly—I've used it many times. So you should get your coat and leave."

Out in the hall, I couldn't believe it. *She* kicked *me* out!

In the hall, the smell was even worse for some reason. I pulled my shirt up high to cover my nose, and waited for the elevator, fuming. She'd gotten it all wrong! She was the lousy date, not me!

—Ken, 28, political consultant, Minneapolis

✳   ✳   ✳

My sister was the usual receptacle for my laments. I was telling her about my last date. "A total slob. Let me put it this way," I told her, redoing her eye shadow, "he had so many fruit flies swarming around his trash that I needed an *Out of Africa* hat with a mosquito net veil thing if I went into the kitchen, okay? Get my drift?"

Usually my sister nodded along, clucking her tongue sympathetically, not really listening, which was okay with me, because when she talked she sounded like Rosie Perez, but without the charm or the smarts or the looks. My sister was an aspiring actress, though I told my friends she was mostly a Rosie Perez wannabe—it was that transparent. I was not really interested in anything she had to say. You know what I'm saying?

But that particular time, my sister kind of came out of her coma and said, "Hey, you know somtin? I've got the altuhnative kine a guy fuh ya. Hansome, smart, and tidy-tidy-tidy. I wook wid duh guy. Duh only ting he don't do is use a ruler to measure duh precise distance from duh front of his desk to duh front of duh chair duh visitor sits in. But don't get me wrong, he's not a frick or anyting."

It was with that ringing endorsement from my sister—who had never offered to fix me up before, probably because she was secretly happy that my love life was always sucking eggs while hers was always skipping along merrily, but with total bores, mind you—that I went along with the fix-up.

The guy's name was Mario, and he was the new manager of the messenger service where my sister was the receptionist.

He had called me, and I accepted a date to go to his house for dinner. I figured it was okay to go to his house on our first date because, as I told him on the phone, "If you try any funny stuff, my sister and the guys at her office will break both your arms and your legs, too. Ha ha. Just kidding."

It was love at first sight for me and Mario's house. Some shingle job, but the yard was the eye-catcher. It was as neat as a pin, had flower beds on both sides of the sidewalk and hanging baskets all over the tiny front porch. There were two tall green conelike little green trees on either side of the front door, like I'd seen at hotels.

He answered the door, and I figured it was okay to give him a big smile. Why the heck not? He was a lady-killer, all dressed in white, with longish black hair he combed straight back and big brown eyes.

When he gave me a tiny peck on the cheek, I smelled his cologne and thought of those Obsession ads where the shirt-less guy swung the girl in the swimsuit behind him on the bucking white horse, and I always thought, Aren't her thighs going to chap? How did she swing up there without getting her legs kicked by the horse's feet? And what was she going to hold onto, since the guy wasn't wearing a shirt? And why wasn't he wearing a shirt? Who showed up for horseback rid-ing without a shirt or shoes?

Something also smelled wonderful in the house.

"Hope you like roast chicken with rosemary and garlic," he says.

Nice. A guy who didn't think that chicken was in the wimp section of the meat department.

I followed Mario into his kitchen and he motioned to the kitchen table and said, "Why don't you have a seat? I'm run-ning a little behind schedule. I was late getting home from work."

"So tell me," I said, seizing the moment. "How terrible is my sister at her job? You can tell me."

I smiled at him, hoping that he'd actually give me a tidbit of real work dirt on my sister that I could use against her later.

Mario was transforming before my eyes. He pulled a surgi-cal mask over his head, letting it dangle under his chin. He shoved elbow-length turquoise plastic gloves over his hands and arms, flashed me a smile that would make Tom Cruise jealous, then pulled the mask over his mouth and nose and dropped to his knees.

He was calm, and I was calm. If my sister told him to do

this just so they'd have something to laugh about at work the next day, they could throw this laugh right out the window. I never backed away from an interesting sexual experience with someone I thought I could get to know.

Mario held up a thick roll of packing tape, then ripped it against the perforated edge on the dispenser.

I wondered what the tape was for, and my imagination got going.

Mario took the piece of tape and ran it along the floor.

That was a comedown.

He ripped another piece off the roll, and did the same.

I looked around. Everything in the kitchen was white, even the floor. Even Mario. If not for the gloves and mask, he'd blend right in.

"*What* are you doing?" I asked.

"I had these tiles special-ordered for me," he said, his voice muffled behind the mask. "Sweeping and mopping doesn't get them clean. It just makes the dust and hairs fly around. But if I run tape over each tile, I can get them spotless."

"Fascinate me some more," I said, counting the tiles. "How much did you get done before I got here?"

"I just got started," he said.

I took a paperback out of my handbag, comparing Mario, in his surgical/sports attire, to the picture of Fabio on the cover, staring down the cleavage of a femme in a pink satin gown that looked like it was going to drop to her waist any second. I was on Chapter Three, and so far the pirate/duke hadn't used any tape to clean his floors.

After ten minutes, the sound of the tape ripping off the roll was making my teeth hurt, so I went to the living room. When I heard him exclaim, "Done!", I put Fabio facedown on my handbag and said, "Thank goodness. I'm thirsty."

I was about to step into the kitchen, but he held out his hand to stop me. He pushed my kitchen chair back into precisely the exact position I'd found it in—with the seat about three inches from the edge of the table—and said, "Just one more thing. You can watch, if you like, but from the doorway. I like to bring out the sheen of the floor."

"How do you do that?" I asked, thinking how I'd like to kill my sister. She'd known what she was setting me up with. A swarm of fruit flies would have made me very happy right about then.

"I use a chamois skin to buff each tile with this solution I sent away for. Wait till you see the difference."

Fifteen minutes later, after he'd only massaged the tenth tile, I said, "You know what? I can see that you take this floor very seriously, and I can see why, because it's beautiful. It's okay for a floor to mean a lot to a person. And you know what? I think I'll take a rain check on the dinner, and let you finish up at your own speed. I don't want to rush you or anything. What do you think? Hello, do you hear me down there?"

He jerked off his mask and said, "Great! Call me later, and we'll set something up! Can you see the difference between these tiles and the rest of the floor?"

Later? There would be a later only if I came over in surgical scrubs with those little hospital paper booties, wearing a hair net, and carting a bucket or two of cleaning supplies.

What did I tell my sister? The truth. When I walked in our front door, she looked like she'd won a game show and said, "Home suh early!"

I tried to look sheepish and said, "Yeah, I'm exhausted. You were right. It was instant chemistry. We did things on his kitchen floor I've never done before. I hope he doesn't talk about it at work. I owe you one."

—Celia, 21, makeup artist, New Jersey

* * *

"Can we just swing by Heavenly Peace on the way to dinner?" she asked, checking her lipstick in the side mirror of my car.

It was our first date.

I said, "Isn't Heavenly Peace a funeral home?"

She said, "Yeah. It's the biggest one in the area, so I guess you'd know it!"

It wasn't a place I hung out at.

"Do you mind if I ask why?"

She said, "My aunt's dry cleaner died, and he used to be at all their parties. I just need to swing by, pay my respects, take a peek in the coffin, and I'll be back in a jiffy. Hey, I'm sorry! I didn't mean to be so rude. You can come in with me if you want!"

—Neil, 25, public relations, Houston

✳ ✳ ✳

Dinner was in the style of "design it yourself." That was a first, and last, for me.

I met Luke at my friend's birthday party, and there was a little bit of electricity between us, even in a hot, crowded apartment. He was an artist, he said, and lived downtown. I gave him my phone number.

He called and invited me to dinner at his place Saturday night, and I asked if I could bring anything. He said, "No, I have everything. It's sort of a designer dinner. You'll see."

I was amused; at least he wasn't run-of-the-mill.

His apartment wasn't ordinary, either. Luke answered the door wearing gray overalls, gray T-shirt, and gray sneakers. I felt flashy in my red plaid shirt and blue jeans.

I stepped into an all-black apartment—the walls and floor were black. There were a few touches of gray—for color. And there wasn't one stick of furniture.

"No furniture?" I asked, before I could stop myself.

"Yes, there is," Luke said, motioning toward a huge gray rock. All the rocks were big, two or three feet in diameter, and gray, placed all over the floor. "Try out this one. It's the most comfortable."

I did, trying to be game.

"This is an adventure!" I said, buoying my spirits.

Luke appeared with a gray tray and said, "Have an appetizer."

On the tray were little silver sardines on gray napkins.

He reappeared with a blender full of a gray substance. He poured two glasses full, handing me one, and said, "Try it. It's cucumber, vodka, food coloring, and a few other things I mixed up special."

I took a sip, and it was surprisingly refreshing, if depressing-looking, and put it aside.

Luke said, "Oh, I forgot something. Atmosphere."

He plugged a cord into the wall, and on burst a mile of skull-shaped lights he had strung across the top of the walls. He turned off the overhead light, and the skulls started to blink.

Luke pushed a huge, wide rock in front of me to make a table, and dinner began.

He presented me with black construction paper, crayons, scissors, and a spool of tape, and said, "You have to make your own napkin before you can eat. Make sure it's interesting, or you'll have to start over."

I was a little unnerved, but I decided to turn this weirdness into a challenge, constructing what I thought was a perfect bat.

"Sucks," Luke said, returning from the kitchen. "Start again."

Miffed, I made a second napkin, which I announced was a coffin.

"No way," said Luke, handing me more paper. "Try again."

This time, I said, "That's enough napkin-making for me. Let's eat or I'm going home," and I smiled.

I had to decorate each course using black strands of squid-ink pasta, pieces of black mushrooms, or, during dessert, slivers of chocolate. Naturally, every course was black, from black licorice for a first course to black sea bass and seaweed for the entree, followed by a blackout chocolate cupcake and black coffee in a black mug.

It was delicious, but all the black motifs were making me feel melancholy. I kept thinking back to *Sleepless in Seattle,* when Rita Wilson starts to cry describing the plot of *An Affair to Remember.* Suddenly I remembered a friend from college who'd died in a car crash late at night, and I saw flashes of those Save the Children kids, adorable children with dirt-smudged cheeks and big liquid eyes, particularly one recent shot of a little girl with big black eyes and brown hair who seemed to need me. I bit my bottom lip so I wouldn't cry.

"There's more," announced Luke, presenting a slab of black bread he'd shaped into an alligator, using licorice jelly beans to make the eyes. "This is for tomorrow's breakfast. Let's finish decorating it. Use these flecks of chocolate for the scales on its back, and this rope licorice to get creative."

Breakfast? There wasn't going to be any breakfast with him. Even if I liked him—which I didn't—it would be like sleeping in a morgue.

I stood, dabbed my eyes, and said, "This was a great dinner. Thanks a million, but I'm feeling a little low," and reached for my bag.

Luke said, "Wait. I thought you'd help me rearrange the furniture. I can't do it by myself, it's too heavy. It takes two people."

Help him push around all those huge rocks? Who was he kidding? No way.

I pushed two rocks with him and called it a night, letting myself enjoy a good cry all the way home.

—Cheryl, 26, computer systems analyst, Seattle

✳ ✳ ✳

Christy Turlington could have been *her* sister. Ruby looked just like her.

We met in the waiting room of our dentist, and exchanged numbers.

Each of our dates was better than the one before. After five, she still wouldn't let me past the good-night kiss stage. I respected that.

On our sixth date, I braved torrential rains and a flood warning to get to Ruby's house for dinner.

When I finally arrived, I tried to give her a kiss hello, but she pulled back.

She'd made a great coq au vin, which I devoured, and we sat on her sofa finishing the bottle of wine.

I tried to kiss her again, and this time Ruby got up and handed me my raincoat and umbrella.

I said, "What's the problem?"

She said, "I don't like you. I never did. I only like French men and French food."

I said, "I'm thinking, then, that it's a good idea for us to split up." I would rather go down in history as the dumper, not the dumpee.

I wondered if I had tricked her into wanting me back.

She opened the door, the flood rains blowing through, and said, "Okay. Split."

—Warren, 32, motivational trainer, Arkansas

✳   ✳   ✳

Ronald sold real estate in New York City, so I expected him to live in a glorious steal of a deal. For our third date, he'd asked me to meet at his apartment. He'd kept saying, "It's nothing special," so I knew it had to be magnificent.

He buzzed me into his building, and I climbed the stairs to the fifth floor. I was breathless by the time I knocked on his door. No answer. I knocked again. I leaned my ear to the door; someone was in there. I banged on the door.

I heard footsteps, then the door opened five inches and Ronald's eyes peered at me over the door chain.

"Kieran? I guess you should come in."

He closed the door after me, and I saw that he was naked except for a skimpy bath towel he'd wrapped around his hips.

"Sorry, I haven't bathed yet," he said.

I realized I was staring at his chest, which was very nice, and gathered my composure.

"Oh. Okay."

"I'll just be a few minutes," he said.

I've been late myself from time to time, and guys were faster about getting ready than women, because they had less to do, so I said, "No problem. I can entertain myself. I'll . . . read the newspaper." I picked up the *New York Times* from a chair and sat down with it.

"Great!" he said.

As soon as I relaxed from the frenzy of our greeting, I noticed that the place was a dump. It was dark, lit like a basement, and gloomy. The few pieces of furniture were dark and mismatched.

Ronald went straight to the dining room table and grasped the side of it, which I thought was weird, and magically lifted up the tabletop and stood it against the wall.

"Voilà!" he said, without looking at me. Under the tabletop was a bathtub.

I was in a studio apartment, I suddenly understood.

Ronald gave me a curious look, and I understood that, too. I swiveled sideways and lifted the newspaper in front of my face. I heard him run the water and then get in the tall old tub.

I could hear him splashing around, and I figured it was safe to lower my newspaper. I had two brothers, so the situation didn't perturb me much.

"Interesting arrangement," I said, fishing for details.

"Thanks!" he said, soaping an armpit. "It's dirt cheap! It's one of those real old apartments where everything is literally in one room. See?"

I looked. The sink, stove, toilet, and mini-fridge were lined along one wall. The sheet hanging out of the bottom of his decrepit old sofa was a clue that it was a pullout bed.

Ronald flicked his hand. "When the toilet seat is down, it serves as a dining chair. Pretty inventive, huh?"

Sure was. A little too inventive for me. Problems of logistics were going through my head. If one were to stay over, I wondered, how would one handle some delicate issues of necessary privacy?

Ronald sank into the tub, disappearing, coming up to vigorously shake his head back and forth. He looked boyish and handsome, and I felt a tingle shoot down my chest. I could overlook this creepy place.

I lifted my newspaper, and heard him splashing around.

The sound of profusely dripping water told me that he had stood up in the tub.

"Let's get a move on!" I said, wondering if I should wait in the hall, and beginning to feel irritable. How much more leisurely could his actions get? "Our reservations are in fifteen minutes."

I lowered my newspaper again, and witnessed an eye-popping sight: With the same skimpy towel around his hips, he was standing in the tub, and was able to open the refrigerator door and take out a bottle of wine. He flipped down the toilet seat and put the wine bottle on it. He reached to a shelf for a corkscrew and two glasses and put them on the toilet, too.

"That's the benefit of having a small pad," he said, facing me, beaming, still in the tub. "Not many people have that luxury. Everything is compact in here. While I get dressed, why don't you pour us some wine?" He stepped out of the tub and walked to a small armoire in the corner.

I was thinking, *No way, not since the corkscrew is touching your toilet seat.*

How was I going to sidestep this offer?

He called out, "Let's not go out tonight. I thought I'd cook dinner. I bought spaghetti fixings."

I remembered him saying that when the toilet seat was down, that would be a dining chair. Could I stomach that? I glanced at his long legs disappearing into a pair of jeans. Maybe.

But my eyes zeroed in on the toilet, which was between the fridge and the ministove, and the relationship of those three objects was like a starting gun for me. Too weird.

Without a word, I grabbed my backpack, flung open his apartment door, bolted into the hall, and ran down the hall, flying around the landings at the stairwells, almost sliding down the stairs.

I didn't stop when I got to the sidewalk, just ripped open the door to the street. As I tore across the street, I heard Ronald yell, "I can make chicken, too! Come back! You can name the entree! Come back!"

—Kieran, 23, editorial assistant, New York City

＊ ＊ ＊

"So, you're married?" he asked.

I said, "*No!* I'm single. I already told you that."

Our New Year's Eve date had started out well enough, even if it was a blind date.

My friend Ashley was dating a guy named Peter. Ashley brought me, Peter brought Clark, and the four of us were having drinks at a new bar.

Clark was nice-looking, polite, and funny. He was a systems analyst, and Ashley said that he was supersmart. I had thought, *Wow, he's great and available on New Year's Eve? Aren't I lucky!*

Just then he asked, "Are you from around here?"

I replied, "No. I'm from Iowa. I told you."

He asked where I worked, what I did, if I had any brothers or sisters—topics we had already covered.

I was exasperated. But then we all danced, and I put our conversation behind me.

Back in our booth, the subject of sports came up, and I said, "I'd really like to go ice skating this winter."

Clark said, "Oh. You must be a really good ice skater."

I said, "No. I've never worn a pair of skates."

Ashley was telling a story about her first time on skates, and Clark said to me, "I bet you're like a Dorothy Hamill, aren't you?"

I said, "No, I've never skated before."

Peter and Ashley were talking about a song that came on the jukebox, and Clark said to me, "So have you skated since you were a little kid?"

I looked at him and said, "Didn't you hear me? I've never skated before."

For a second, I thought this was some clever routine that Clark was doing. But he was too distracted, never meeting my eyes, always preoccupied, looking around, and seemed entirely serious.

A few minutes later, Clark turned to me and said, "I bet you're a terrific skater."

I just stared at him, my mouth open, and looked at my friend. Ashley was normal, Peter seemed normal, I was pretty sure I was normal, so what was Clark's story? Did he have a learning disability, a hearing problem, an attention deficit? Or was he so bored with me that he wasn't even trying to concentrate?

As if reading my mind Clark said, "Hey, Ashley! Peter! Why didn't someone tell me that your friend here could be in Ice Capades!"

He went on and on about my expert skating ability until I said, "All right, already! I'm not a skater!"

Clark made a disbelieving face, shrugged, and said, "Sorry. I thought you were."

The plans were to reconvene at Peter's house. Clark got in Peter's car, and I got in Ashley's car.

Ashley asked why I looked uptight, and I said, "You're kidding, right? Didn't you notice how Clark didn't listen to a thing I said, and kept repeating himself, asking me the same questions about myself over and over?"

Ashley hadn't noticed, so I told her about the ice skating conversation. We both started laughing.

We were at a red light, and I looked to my right. Peter's car was next to us, and he motioned me to roll down my window. When I did, Clark leaned across Peter and said to me, "What are you girls laughing at? You're laughing at me, aren't you?"

I said, "No! Ashley said something funny, that's all."

Clark said, "What are you girls laughing at? You're laughing at me, aren't you?"

I said, "No! Ashley made a joke that I can't remember now."

Clark said, "Oh, yeah? What are you girls laughing at? You're laughing at me, aren't you?"

Ashley started laughing quietly, and I tried not to.

Clark said, "What are you girls laughing at?"

We were laughing so hard that I started to roll up the window. I must not have been the first date to leave Clark's spaced-out presence and start laughing. This had happened to him before. I only had an inch or two left before the window was rolled shut, and through that little crack I heard Clark yell, "You're laughing at me, aren't you?"

—Tara, 25, loan processor, Alaska

* * *

"Run that by me again?" I asked.

She repeated, "I'm not at the point in my life where I can allow myself to be happy." But she was smiling.

I'd been off balance all night. I'd taken her dancing, and she'd spent most of the time accepting drinks I bought for her, and dancing with a guy she said she was just friends with. After thirty minutes of this, I headed for the door. She came running after me, saying, "Please don't leave. I didn't think you liked to dance! That guy is just a good friend. Don't be mad."

I said, "I'm not a fool! I'm spending money on you, and you're dancing with someone else! You're treating me like dirt, and I don't need that. So long."

She apologized some more, which I had to give her credit for. I made my point to her again. And, to be honest, I liked that she was kissing my ass; I enjoyed it.

We went to another club, danced twice, and I tried to kiss her. She put her hand on my chest and said something about not allowing herself to be happy.

I said, "What does that mean? You look happy to me."

She sighed and said, "Tonight, what was your favorite part? Was it picking me up? Or going to the club? Or dancing just now? Or was it feeling your blood boil when I kept dancing with that guy? Didn't it feel out-of-body when I ran after you and you told me how mad you were? Didn't it feel great when I said I was sorry, and we drove over here? Wasn't it more of a special night than if everything had gone as expected? Don't you find that those smooth-going nights are boring compared to this?"

She said some more, but I had stopped listening and started thinking, *Here's another loony tune I was attracted to.*

Looking serious, she explained, "Whenever I get happy, I torture and punish myself in some mental way so that I can be miserable. And you wanted to kiss me just now and I wanted to kiss you back—but I couldn't go on like that with you. I think that we shouldn't see each other again."

I said, "Okay. Let me drive you home." She wasn't going to get an argument from me.

On the way to her apartment she said, "You're upset, aren't you? I'm sorry. Listen, call me when you get home, and call me when you get up in the morning, will you? Promise you'll call me. Do you want to come upstairs and have a drink with me? Why not? How do you feel? Do you want to know how I feel?"

With my car idling in front of her apartment, I thought hard for a graceful way out of this and a way to get her out of my car.

I said, "Do you know how I feel? I feel really, really happy. Jubilant, elated, in fact. And you look radiant."

She threw her hands to her cheeks in horror and said, "I've got to go. Goodbye."

—Zach, 35, fireman, New Mexico

❋ ❋ ❋

Blitzing, that's what I was doing. I was going on dates, any dates, with just about anyone. I had decided to follow all the dating advice in magazines and books.

I wasn't going to be picky. I was going to let everyone I knew know that I wanted to be set up on a date. I wasn't going to have any expectations. I wasn't going to compare one date to another—or to my fantasy of the right man.

I would, however, enjoy the evening for what it was. I would relish the opportunity to meet a new person. I might discover I was out with a new business contact or a brand-new friend. I was energized, organized, optimistic, outgoing, and upbeat. I was blitzing.

After my seventh blind date, I was no long blitzing. I was fritzing, going on the blink. I was tired of my own small talk, tired of their small talk. I was ready to go back to the two-blind-dates-a-year pattern I'd been on. Then my friend Julie called and said that I had to psych up again because she had a blind date for me.

Julie had met the corporate tax attorney of her dreams, and

he had a colleague who needed fixing up. We'd all double-date.

"I've got it all figured," Julie said. "We'll go to a comedy club so that no one has to do much talking. You'll have just enough interaction to tell if you want to go out again or not. And it'll be guaranteed fun. Let's do it."

I hadn't been to a comedy club in years, so I agreed. The plan was that I would meet the three of them at the club.

At the door of the comedy club, I saw Julie animatedly waving her hand from a table that was dead center in the room.

"Great table!" I said.

Julie's date was what I expected. His friend wasn't. My date was 5'3", and weighed about 250 pounds. That didn't bother me too much—I had relatives with that same body shape. What bothered me was the badger living on top of his head. There was some clump, a pile, really, of Brillo pads that was slightly off kilter.

"I'm Harry," he said, shaking my hand with one hand and adjusting his clump with the other.

I reviewed my goals. Upbeat, outgoing, just out for a pleasant night. Maybe he was interesting.

"We were just talking about how we pulled off a doozy of a win for a company that wanted to retain nonprofit status but the community suspected it wasn't. We saved the company."

"Well, was it really nonprofit?" I asked, ordering a beer.

"Heck no!" Harry bellowed. "That's the beauty of it. We're celebrating tonight!" He and his friend clinked glasses, while Julie beamed.

The lights went down, and I checked my watch. I was fritzing again, wanting to be home with my cats and a video.

The first comic was good. He unhooked his microphone from the stand and started roaming the room, making nasty but funny cracks about some of the patrons. His eyes hit Harry, and you could see that his eyes had hit a slot machine jackpot. He zoomed over to us, stood staring at Harry. We all tensed. Then the comic walked away, picking on a woman's hat behind us. Whew.

The second comic said, "Haircuts! They can cost ya, can't they? Why not just shave your head and get it over with and get a toupee? Maybe wear a bad one. Like that guy over there."

He pointed at Harry, jumped down off the stage, and strode toward us. I thought we were all four going to die. People around us looked at Harry's head and started to titter. Then the comic walked right past us, needling a guy behind us who had his own hair but had a lousy style.

The third and fourth comics made hair jokes. They would hover around Harry, all four of our stomachs would knot, then they'd move on.

It took me a while to catch on. The fact that each one singled out Harry and then moved on was a running gag, and was going to be a running gag through the night.

Harry was smiling gamely, adjusting his toupee from time to time. Once he shouted to me, "That's some act, isn't it?"

The fifth comic circled us, circled us again, his face screwed up in thought. He stopped, put his hand to his forehead, thought some more, then looked up and yelled into his mike, "Nah-ah-ah. I can't." Then he walked away.

When the show was over, Harry said, "That was great! I thought they were going to say something about my hair, didn't you? That's why I love going to comedy clubs all the time. I feel like a star." He turned to his friend and said, "Remember the one we went to last weekend? The guy put my toupee on his head and wore it for his act. It was great. Say, are you free next weekend? Let's go to another one!"

—Lorraine, 37, dermatologist, Chicago

* * *

Alarm clocks drive me crazy. I can't stand the grating, whizzing sound. I get up on my own, at five in the morning, on the dot.

The first night I stayed over at my new girlfriend's apartment, I fell into bed but couldn't sleep. Neither of us was a big drinker, but that night we'd had enough liquor for four people. I was feeling queasy and hoped I could sleep in. I don't think I fell asleep until two in the morning.

It seemed like only a matter of minutes.

Alarms were going off all over the bedroom. I thought we were in a three-alarm fire or something, and pressed my hands over my ears in an effort to stop the lightning bolts in my forehead from shooting around behind my eyeballs. I was hurting.

I sat up and watched my girlfriend switch off the alarm clock on her side of the bed. It was six in the morning. She hopped out of bed to switch off the alarm clock on her bureau. There was a clock on her mini-TV, under her bed, on her desk, and in her closet.

"Make it stop!" I yelled in agony.

"There are three more! I can't remember where I hid them! Where does it sound like they're coming from?"

I put my head under my pillow and folded the sides around my ears, but I couldn't muffle the shrill, grating screams of the alarm clocks.

One at a time, the last three alarms went quiet, and silence came like a miracle. My heart was pounding and my head was throbbing. I couldn't move.

My girlfriend said, "Sorry about that. I have trouble getting up in the morning for work, so I stash a bunch of alarm clocks all over the place to force me to get out of bed and stay out of bed long enough to be completely awake. Last night I must have forgotten this was Saturday, and I set them all."

Oh my gosh. If we continued dating, I'd have this cacophonous wake-up call to look forward to every morning? I couldn't bear one alarm, but with this girl, we'd be hunting down clocks for a good five minutes every morning. I actually thought I might cry. What a nightmare. She was perfect in every way, except for this.

I relaxed and tried to ignore the drums in my head. She cuddled me, and the world felt right again. It wasn't that bad, now that it was over. And if she needed that racket to get out of bed, who was I to sabotage it? I could wean her down to two, I was sure. Everything would be okay.

Then, pow! Pow! Pow! Pow-pow-pow! The alarms went off again like machine-gun fire. One started, two seconds later the next chimed in, a few seconds later the next started, until all nine or ten alarm clocks were bellowing like a horrible orchestra of torture.

"I'm sorry!" she yelled over the racket. "I guess I hit the snooze buttons instead of the off buttons! It's just habit! I usually hit the snooze buttons on the clocks at least three times before I get up!"

Oh no.

—Ed, 28, rancher, Wyoming

* * *

When he took the eyedropper out of the inside pocket of his suit jacket, I couldn't stop staring. He continued talking, but I was mesmerized.

It was our first date. We were at a cozy little Italian restaurant, and we had ordered about fifteen minutes earlier.

I was working at an advertising agency. He owned several fast food chains and was one of our biggest accounts. The chemistry had been flying between us for over a year, and this afternoon he had asked if I wanted to join him for dinner.

With the eyedropper in his hand, he continued to talk casually about America's new appreciation for spicy food.

He reached into his pocket again, and this time pulled out a small green vial. He dipped the eyedropper into the vial, filled it, then squeezed it over his water glass. Several drops plopped into his water, turning his water green.

I didn't want to be rude, so I didn't ask what he was doing.

He lifted the glass, and it wobbled. His hand was shaking so much that he barely got the glass to his lips, and he drank the green liquid in eight starts and stops. His shirt collar looked damp—he was sweating profusely.

He used both hands to set the glass on the table, steadied it, and said, "That was a muscle relaxant. I have a problem eating in front of other people. I get extremely uptight."

I nodded, looking him square in his terrified eyes, and hopefully made him feel less uncomfortable by saying, "Okay . . ."

Well, the muscle relaxant must not have had time to kick in, because he was fighting his salad. He'd spear a clump of leaves, then he'd lift his fork, which was shaking wildly, trying to aim it at his mouth, talking all the while about the new ethnicity of food trends.

It looked like the Invisible Man had grabbed my date's wrist and was trying to wrestle his hand down to the table while he was trying to battle the fork to his mouth.

He would get close, then the fork would veer crazily to the left, then to the right, then down, then up, then down, and —he stabbed his left cheek with his fork.

I grimaced, he grimaced, then he yanked away the fork, quickly shoved the food in his mouth, wrenched out the fork, and had combat with the Invisible Man, who was trying to stop him from lowering the fork to his salad plate.

He harpooned a second forkful of salad, glared intently at the fork as if he were thinking, "This time, I'm gonna do it!" then had the same struggle, ending by forking his left cheek again. We continued to talk, with me saying, "For instance, some catsup now comes with salsa added in . . ."

When the waiter cleared our salad plates, my date had fork marks all over his face, salad strewn on the table and on the floor. He had taken off his jacket, and his shirt was plastered to his chest from perspiration.

When the waiter served my plate of lasagna and his plate of spaghetti, I almost groaned. Spaghetti? He ordered spaghetti? My heart started pounding on his behalf.

Spaghetti sauce was flying, his fork hand was dancing all over the air in front of his face, tendrils of spaghetti were flapping in the wind. He smashed the fork into his other cheek, then jammed the spaghetti into his mouth, long strands hanging limply out of his mouth as he took a second to catch his wind before sucking them up. His eyes were open wide—he was concentrating.

People at the tables nearby were staring at us, which made me nervous. So I wound up imitating him, though in my own fashion. I was so self-conscious that I dropped a piece of lasagna on my lap. Another piece fell apart on its way to my mouth, disintegrating all over the tablecloth.

A forkful of spaghetti sauce splattered across my face as my date was boxing the air with his fork. He asked the shocked waiter for more napkins, and we were given a stack.

No wonder he specialized in fast food restaurants. He could stand in a corner or eat in his car, unseen, and messily—but quickly—wolf down an item in privacy.

I went blind! No, it was just gobs of sauce that had landed in my eyes.

My face, bangs, and shirt were covered with his spaghetti sauce. My lap was full of lasagna. Our table was one red and green dump from his sauce and salad. Only a quarter of the way through my lasagna, I stopped eating and tucked a napkin in my shirt collar, wishing I could tie a napkin around my head and hold another one over my face while we talked.

He never stopped eating. It took a solid hour, but he brawled his way through the entire plate of spaghetti, splashing himself, me, and the white-shirted back of a man nearby.

He jousted his last forkful into his mouth, strained to get the fork back on the table, and said, "Made it!"

I couldn't bear to look at him. His hair, face, shirt, arms, and hands were covered with sauce and bits of spaghetti. His face was pocked with fork marks. At last that was over—and so was any chance of romance.

I signaled for the waiter—I wanted our check. Enough of this torture, and of this mess.

When the waiter appeared my date said, "How about dessert and coffee?" and the waiter spoke for me when he said, "*Signore,* are you sure?"

I breathed a sigh of relief, but my date said, "Absolutely! Bring us two coffees and a dessert list! The night's not over yet!"

—Delia, 23, advertising, Boston

4

* * * *

Bad Beginnings

Whoa! What brought that on? How did this date shatter so fast? It was over before it even had a chance to get going. Let's start again! On second thought, let's not.

Strategy, strategy—that was how we had to land babes. My bud George and I were just starting out. We were eighteen and had just gotten the courage to be bold with women.

We did it like this: We'd spot two cute chicks walking along, then we'd follow them, hanging back at first, then getting closer and closer. Maybe stopping to stare in the same store windows that they did, until one of us—preferably one of them—would say, "Hey, not you again! This is funny! Where are you guys heading?" Then we'd offer to buy them a coffee. Usually we'd wind up trying to *badger* them into having coffee with us—not that that ever worked.

That night, we saw two babes our age up ahead on Columbus Avenue. We followed our plan. At the second store window that we all four just happened to stop at together, George said, "Hey, not—" but the two girls spotted us and took off before we could close in.

"You must have scared them off. You sounded like you were going to mug them," I said, hitting him hard on the arm. "You're a jerk."

George said, "You're the jerk. Let's go!"

We went as fast as we could without actually breaking into a run. The girls would look back over their shoulders from time to time, see us, and speed up.

They made a quick left turn, hoping to throw us off. But we were on top of the situation.

George said, "Let's go up a block, then take a left. Hurry!"

We ran up one block, turned left, and ran to the end of that block, then turned right and walked slowly.

Bingo.

I said, "Chick alert at seven o'clock."

George, supercool, barely nodded. We positioned ourselves in front of a store that had bath soaps and perfumes and other girl stuff, and pretended to be busy looking inside.

It couldn't have gone better if we'd had divine intervention.

The two chicks bumped into *us*. George and I tried to look annoyed, and one of the girls said, "I'm sorry. It's just that these two dweebs were following us, and we're trying to ditch them and weren't watching where we were going."

Still going by the game plan, I said, "Are you all right? Did they try to hurt you?" I felt like a sleaze when I said that, but I felt that saying it was key.

"No," said the other girl. "We're okay. They were harmless. Just a couple of pinheads. You should have seen them."

George and I tensed, then remembered the goal. The goal was not to say, "We're those pinheads." The goal was to buy them coffee, get their phone numbers, and go on an actual date before we were ninety.

George said, "Bummer. Maybe you should walk with us for a few blocks and tell us if you see them. We'll take care of them for you."

One of the girls said, "We don't need protection, but we'll walk a little ways with you."

It was time to get a date going, so I said, "We're going in here to have café au lait. Want to join us?"

One girl said, "Sure!"

The other girl said, "Hey, wait a minute! I thought you looked familiar. You're the two jerks who were following us, aren't you? You're the guys."

Her friend took a close look and said, "I can't believe this. You're following us and playing games like we're a couple of fools," and they huffed away.

George yelled after them, "Yeah, well at least I'm not a pinhead!" and walked in a tight circle, kicking at the pavement.

And that was how we landed our babes.

—Will, 35, doctor, New York City

* * *

Nature was not one of my favorite things. I liked indoor houseplants, I liked little hikes, I liked sweeping vistas. But I didn't like long walks in the woods followed by camping out.

But the guy I was interested in, William, was a nature lover, and I made the mistake of trying to impress him by saying that I was, too.

That's how, on our first date, we wound up in the woods, hiking with heavy backpacks. He had planned three days and two nights in a wilderness area that was his favorite. In fact, he spent every weekend camping, often flying to another state if he needed better weather, and said he was glad to find a woman who could go with him.

There was one other white lie. William thought my eyes were gorgeous. What he didn't know was that my deep blue eyes were usually a pale blue-gray—the great color was due to my new colored contact lenses. I didn't tell him, though. If that was the feature he liked best about me, I sure wasn't going to ruin a possible romance by showing him the real things.

Climbing up some absurd embankment, one of my contacts fell out. Immediately the world went crazy. Without contacts, I was so nearsighted that it wasn't funny. One lens in and one out was not going to work. I took out the other contact, and it slipped and fell into a bed of leaves.

My heart sank. Not only would he see that my eyes were not Caribbean blue, he'd see that I was blind as a bat.

I could barely see him up ahead, and I hurried to catch up. I looked like I was vogueing, putting my arms akimbo, reaching out one foot to find solid ground, probably walking in circles for a while. He came up beside me, and I clutched his arm to steady myself.

"Feeling sexy?" he asked.

How could anyone feel amorous in the woods, unable to see, with any number of rocks around to fall on? I lowered my eyelids so we couldn't have eye contact and said, "Yes. I love it here. I'm having an absolutely wonderful time."

That's when I walked right into a tree. I hit it so hard that my arms went around the tree and I sort of slid down it a few feet. I had a bloody nose and a gash over my eye.

When we made camp, I laid down and held a compress over my eyes. Finally William demanded a look, and when he peered into my one unswollen eye, he said, "Hey. Wait a minute. Something's different."

I said, "It's night. Colors are dim in the dark."

He shined a flashlight on my face, examining my gash and the eye that was swollen shut, then beamed my open eye and said, "Colored contacts, huh?"

I nodded.

He switched off the flashlight and said, "You hate camping, right?"

I nodded again and said, "This gash hurts pretty bad. I don't think I can make it for another two days camping. I want to go home."

In the morning, we hiked back to the car. I knew it was an inconvenient twist to his plans, he wouldn't have time to go back and pick up where he left off, but I'd had enough of the woods, and I was pretty sure I needed a doctor.

If William ever asked me if I liked to go hunting, I'd tell him the truth. Probably.

—Patty, 31, lie detector analyst, Colorado

* * *

Strategy, strategy—we'd perfected it to such an extent that George and I were surprised when it struck out three times.

We were eighteen, and we were taking our strategy out for a walk again tonight.

I said, "Babe alert. Eleven o'clock. Chickeroonies."

George said, "Oh-oh yeah. You got that right."

We did the first window-shopping bit, stopping at the same storefront as the girls, then we did it a second time at another window.

I said, "Hey! It's you two again! You're following us."

Instead of saying, "Get lost," the one with blond hair down to her waist said, "Yes! It's you! What a coincidence! How funny!"

Yes, wasn't it! It was great! They said they'd love to have a decaf cappuccino with us.

At the coffee shop, they said they only had ten minutes, but that was ten more than we'd ever gotten before, so it sounded like a gold mine situation to us.

They sucked down their coffees while George and I sipped ours, hoping to stretch the ten into fifteen.

"Well, we've got to go!" said the one I had my eye on.

So fast? We were just getting started.

I said, "Why don't we exchange numbers?" We were eighteen years old and we were getting lucky!

She said, "Sure! That'd be great!"

Was I hearing things?

She reached into her backpack and handed out three pieces of paper and three pens. We exchanged numbers. I looked at the piece of paper she'd handed me. What was this, hieroglyphics?

"Where do you two live?" asked George, turning his paper over in puzzlement.

"Norway!" said mine. "We leave early tomorrow, and we have to pack tonight. You're such nice guys!"

That explained why we'd gotten lucky. They didn't know how to size up American guys yet.

I said, "So what does this mean?"

She said, "You'll probably never see us again! But we can be pen pals!"

We held on to their numbers and addresses for a couple of blocks, then threw them out.

Our first breakthrough was eleven minutes with two girls who were heading off to a place near the North Pole.

We still weren't doing so well.

—Will, 35, doctor, New York City

* * *

Not bad! I looked at my reflection in the mirror. My blind date would be happy to see me.

I answered the door, handed him a glass of wine, sat beside him on the sofa, crossing my legs in my new green mini-dress, and said, "Tell me about this restaurant we're going to."

He stared at my legs. I was pleased. My legs were my best feature.

He said, "Is there anything you want to tell me? Like, do you feel okay?"

"What? Sure! What are you talking about?"

He pointed to my legs.

"You're sick. Why aren't you talking about it? Your legs—I can see the lesions from here."

"Lesions?" I looked at my legs in horror, but didn't see anything. "I don't have any lesions. You're seeing things."

He looked upset. He clumped his wineglass on my coffee table and said, "Oh, no. You've got them up and down your legs."

"Where?" I yelled, worried that I had symptoms of AIDS.

"There!" he yelled, pointing. "And there! And there! And there!"

He backed out of my house, his eyes tearing up, and saying, "I'm sorry. I have two friends who just died from this, and I just got divorced, and I don't want any more unhappy times right now. It's too soon. I'm sorry," and he left.

As he was backing out of my driveway, I opened the door and said, "Wait! These are patterned stockings! My hose are flesh-colored with little light green dots on them! Wait!"

It was a shame. He was cute.

—Bernadette, 36, doctor of family medicine, Utah

✳ ✳ ✳

Rita agreed to meet me for drinks.

It was 1993. I met her in the laundry room of our apartment building, and had started talking about how slow the dryers were. I'd asked for her number, she'd given it to me, and I'd called her at work to ask her out for a drink.

Since we lived in the same building and would run into each other regardless of whether our encounter was good or bad, I wanted neutral ground where nothing could go wrong.

I sat at the bar, waiting. When she entered, she joined me, suggesting we stay at the bar instead of getting a table.

She ordered a whiskey and immediately said, "This will

probably lead to a date. So I want to know. What's your political standing?"

I was thinking that I loved her smile. Politics?

I said, "Well, I voted for Clinton. I think we needed a change."

She slammed her glass down onto the bar and said, "Are you a *taxpayer*? Do you know what Clinton is doing to all our incomes? Do you have any idea what he'll do to our taxes? Do you feel like throwing your money away and voting for every Democrat who comes down the pike? You probably don't make much of an income anyway, or you'd care. I'm leaving. I can tell you right now—my future husband and my kids, no one will be a Democrat. I can promise you that. It's people like you who ruin this country."

Then she stormed out.

—Owen, 23, landscape designer, Connecticut

❋ ❋ ❋

Biceps, triceps, delts, abs, quads, he had it all. He was in great shape, nice-looking, funny, and a great dancer, even if he was extremely quiet.

The previous weekend, my college suitemate and I had gone to a local nightclub, and two older guys started dancing with us. They liked to dance, too, and we all exchanged phone numbers. They had called and asked us to meet them at the club tonight.

Around midnight, my "date" asked me if we were hungry. He said we could all four go to the grocery store, and he'd cook breakfast at his place.

My friend and I were famished, and it sounded like a good idea. And at least this way my friend and I could get to know our dates, maybe laying the groundwork to get real dates going in the future, instead of this initial "meet us there" arrangement.

In the car, I was flirting and tossing my hair when I said, "Yeah, but can you cook?"

My date said, "Oh, yeah. I learned how to cook at the Big House."

I said, "I know that place! It's great! I went there with my parents! You're the chef there?"

The two guys exchanged give-me-a-break looks, and my date said, "No. The Big House. As in prison. I worked in the kitchen."

After a pause, my suitemate said, "Oh. You were an employee?"

My date gave my friend and me long looks and said, "No. I was an inmate. Look. You're nice girls, but this isn't going to work out. You're too young for us, and that only leads to trouble."

He made a U-turn, dropping me and my friend at the club.

How's that for a humiliating brush-off? Two dean's list psychology students dumped right off the bat by a pair of ex-cons for not being smart enough for them. That hurt.

—Janie, student, 19, New York

* * *

Piece of cake, that's what I was telling my friends. It was time for me to meet my girlfriend's mother, and I wasn't worried. I had spoken to Heidi's mother, Marta, on the phone a couple of times, and she was as sweet as she could be. Heidi's family was from Germany and I'm German-American, so this would be easy.

Tomorrow was the big day. I was going to pick up Heidi at her family's house. We'd have a drink with her mother, then Heidi and I would continue our date by going out to a movie.

Heidi told me to make sure I looked presentable, and to get a haircut. "It's going to be great," Heidi said, giving me assurance I didn't need. "My mother is going to love you. I've told her all about you, and she says you sound perfect. And she thinks you have a great phone voice, real strong and confident."

Knowing all that, and because I am pretty confident, I didn't bother getting my suit dry-cleaned, and I decided my hair looked fine.

For the dinner date, I wore jeans, a sweater, and a sportcoat. Heidi would be at her mother's house early, waiting for me, and I picked up a bouquet of tulips, her favorite, for her.

I have to admit that I was a little nervous when I knocked on her mother's door. Heidi had promised that she'd answer, so I relaxed.

After a few seconds the door whipped open. An arm reached out and snatched the flowers out of my hand. It was Heidi's mother.

She said, "Oh. For me, I suppose. Thank you."

I didn't correct her, just waited for her to ask me inside.

She studied my face and said, "Oh. You're Rudy? I thought you'd be taller."

I was looking down on her. I'm about 5'10", and she couldn't have been more than five feet. What was she talking about? She had to be getting a crick in her neck from looking up at me.

She spoke again, "I thought you'd be stronger, not so frail. Well, what is there to say?"

She turned and went inside, leaving me in the doorway.

It hasn't gotten much better since.

—Rudy, 29, marketing, Wisconsin

❋ ❋ ❋

Samurai weren't my usual cup of tea. Yet there he was, a blond guy in skimpy gym shorts, socks, and sneakers, with a white and red Japanese warrior scarf tied around his forehead. He wasn't wearing a shirt. He was standing in the lobby of his apartment building executing martial arts moves, making fierce eye contact with everyone who walked in.

As I announced myself to the guy at the front desk, I knew in my heart of hearts that this samurai had to be my blind date. Indeed, the clerk nodded to the samurai and said, "There's your man."

Before I could turn and run, the warrior said, "Sally! Just give me a second."

He swiveled on one foot, spraying an arc of perspiration that caught me full in the face, then halted to confront an older couple with bags of groceries who entered the building and by-passed the front desk.

"Excuse me," he said to them. "You don't live here. You have to announce yourself to the desk."

The couple got bug-eyed. The man said, "We're visiting from Florida. We're staying with our son. He lives in 25D."

The samurai said, "25D. That's where Lyle Anderson lives."

The woman said, "No it isn't. That's where our son Mickey lives."

The samurai glared at them, then said, "Okay. You can go up."

To me, he held out a sweaty palm, and said, "I'm Stanley. Come up."

I had stupidly agreed to have a quick drink with him at his apartment on my way to my sister's for dinner. Our schedules hadn't matched up well for anything else, and I didn't want to commit to an actual date until I'd checked him out first.

In his apartment, I said, "How many people live here?" The little apartment was packed with too much furniture, and portable closets.

"Two, sometimes three," he said, doing some weird moves in front of a full-length mirror on the back of the door.

I stood, clutching my briefcase, and said, "Aren't you an insurance salesman? I didn't know you were into martial arts."

"Just a hobby," he said, thrusting out his chest. "Want a health shake?"

"No," I said. "Just some tap water."

He told me to take a seat on his messy couch, but I stood and mentally rehearsed my parting line, which I'd be using shortly.

He handed me my water, then said, "Listen to this! I just got the new CD."

He put on Pearl Jam, and cranked it so loud that I wanted to cry.

"Turn it down!" I screamed two times before he did.

Then he cocked his head and said, "Did you hear that? I'll be right back."

I hadn't heard a thing.

He whipped open the door. I looked into the hall and saw him disappear behind a door marked "Stairwell A."

He returned in a minute and said, "Can you believe my downstairs neighbors? They're always making a racket like that. Got to keep them in line."

"So, how do you know my sister's boss?" I asked, wanting to nail down this one detail before I exited.

He started to tell me while he picked up two massive free weights and began doing arm curls. He stopped suddenly, dropped the weights to the floor with a thud that made the floor shake, then said, "I'll be right back."

He went down the stairwell, returned, and said, "Can you believe how loud they are? They always play their television at top volume."

I listened. He must have been picking them up on sonar.

He lifted the weights again, and I repeated my question.

He said, "Now I'm getting really ticked off. Can you hear that? They didn't turn down their TV one notch. I'll be right back."

He tossed the weights into a corner, and the floor rumbled.

He stormed back in, saying, "People like them are impossible to live with. You've got to show them who's boss. Listen to that. Do you hear them? This time I'm going to call them and tell them to turn it down. First I'll hang up a few times to make them jumpy. Sit down. I'll be with you in a minute."

He looked across the room, straightening his samurai bandanna in the reflection of one of his mirrors, then dialed the number by heart.

I said, "Sayonara," and walked to the elevator.

From his open doorway, I heard him saying into the phone, "You think you can toy with me? You think I don't have anything better to do than see you or talk to you three or four times a week? I've got a date here, and you're upsetting her. Yeah, you are. And I'm not too happy about it, either."

The elevator opened, and I jumped on, curious to see who lived in the apartment below him, and wondering what they'd have to say about their samurai neighbor. Instead, I pushed the button for the lobby, where I passed the older couple. They were standing at the front desk, asking the clerk if it was all right for them to come and go unannounced or if, as the samurai had instructed them, they needed a pass.

—Sally, 24, human resources, Chicago

* * *

learned two things in my first few months in New York City. I learned about BYOP—bring your own partner—and about moonlight.

Moonlighting had a clear definition for me. I'd get up at seven in the morning to go to work as a bank teller, then race off at five-thirty to a part-time job as a bookkeeper from seven to midnight. I'd moved from Iowa, and had only been in New York three months. I'd been lucky enough to snare both jobs, and, being industrious and thinking I could keep this up indefinitely, I didn't give up either job. February had been tough, but because it was tax time, March and April were grueling—I worked on the bookkeeping full-time on the weekends, some-times from ten in the morning until eleven at night.

So, my first free weekend, a buddy from the bank said, "Hey, you busy Saturday night? Let's go hit some clubs. It's time you let loose."

I couldn't agree more, and was happy when Saturday rolled around. We went uptown to a new club that my friend re-ported was hot, and when an old James Brown tune came blasting on the sound system, I got excited and walked straight to the bar and asked a woman, "Excuse me, would you like to dance?"

She gave me a head-to-toe inspection, grimaced like I had just rolled off a garbage barge, and snorted, "No," and looked away as she blew her cigarette smoke up my nose.

I coughed, said to myself, "Get back in there, man. You've been shot down before," and looked around. I gave my buddy a thumbs-up—I was no quitter—and asked another woman, "Excuse me, pretty lady. Would you care to dance with me?"

I went down the row of women, five of them, and their an-swers went like this: "No." "No." "No." "No." "No." I reeled back, and the fifth woman hopped off her bar stool, pulled down a shiny, tiny gold dress over her thighs, and stalked off. I turned around and said to no one in particular, "Man, I can't believe this."

I looked at the dance floor, and saw a girl dancing by her-self. She looked good, so I hopped right in and started dancing with her. She stopped dancing and walked off the floor. I turned around, and I saw a guy dancing by himself. I thought, "Dude, all you got to do is ask a chick to dance. Pathetic."

I saw five girls dancing in a small circle, their handbags on the floor in the middle of the group. I hopped right in, danc-ing like crazy, so happy to be letting loose and getting into the music. Then I noticed that they were drifting off to the left, so I drifted off to the left with them. I smiled at a girl I liked, and danced closer to her, whereupon she said, "Go away," and the whole group made an abrupt shift to the right, leaving me dancing alone like a fool.

I searched out my buddy, and he said, "Good grief. This is definitely your first time out. The women come here to dance, not to get hit on. You're hassling them, man. Chill."

I thought, "This is very weird." Then I saw two guys, hetero-looking guys, dancing together and I poked my friend and laughed and said, "What are they having, a relationship?"

My friend looked at me like I just crawled out of a hole—I was getting a lot of you-fool looks tonight—and shook his head.

That was my first lesson on going out to find a date in New York City at a normal-looking place where the people look normal: Leave everyone alone. Don't talk to anyone, don't ask anyone to dance, don't offer to buy anyone a drink—ever. If you want to dance and didn't bring a partner with you, dance by yourself. That's when I learned about BYOP, bring your own partner.

Well, after a year, it made sense to me. After getting hassled and jostled by the crowds in the city, people wanted some private, safe space to enjoy themselves, which meant no stranger tapping you or talking to you. If I went to those kinds of clubs without a date, I spent my time getting into my own groove.

About that time, I went back home to Iowa to visit. My best friend said he knew a girl he wanted me to take out—he wanted to double-date. I said no, that I'd just meet him and the two babes there—New York style.

I got to the club and saw my friend across the room, but a tune that came on was so great that I decided I had to dance right then and delay the greeting for a minute or two.

I went straight to the center of the dance floor and started dancing by myself. I was doing mean criss-cross arm movements, jogging big and high in place, using my right arm to crank the air at my side and swivel my feet fast so that my body moved to the side while I was still facing forward. I was so happy to be back home, I closed my eyes and let loose. My first trip back home was off to a great start.

At the end of the song, I straightened up, feeling happy to be alive, and looked around. The floor had cleared. I was the only person standing there, while everyone else was on the sidelines, staring. I waited for the next song to come on, but there wasn't one.

My friend materialized and said, "What the heck are you doing, man?" He looked around sheepishly, as if he were embarrassed to be standing next to me.

I said, "Hey, I was just showing you how we dance in New York."

My friend said, "Yeah, man, but this is Iowa. And that was your date who just walked out the back door. Acclimate."

I thought I was.

—Scott, 31, bank teller, New York City

* * *

Backfired. That's what my big idea did. Backfired right on me, and I was standing there, wearing a tuxedo, with a paper bag on my head, when my blind date opened her door and said, "Hey, there!"

What happened was, my buddy Andy was escorting his girlfriend, Amy, to the Annual Spinsters Ball in San Francisco. The Spinsters Club was some upper-crust organization where women could only be a member by invitation, and had to be from a pillar-of-society family. Since Amy's friend Marty needed a date, Andy said, "Drive up here, and we'll double-date. You can take Marty. The ball is on Saturday night, so we can double-date. And Friday night and Sunday, you and I can tool around. You know, make a weekend of it. It'll be fun!"

I needed an excuse to get me away from my business in La Jolla, so I agreed, getting my tuxedo dry-cleaned, my shoes buffed.

Friday night, out for drinks with Andy and Amy, I said, "Hey Amy, what's Marty like?"

Amy said, "Oh, you're gonna have a lot of fun. She's one of my best friends, and she's a lot of fun."

That sounded like good party material, didn't it? I wouldn't be at a fancy party with a dud on my arm.

Saturday night, ready to go, I realized that this was only my second blind date. My first one had been a complete bust, and I didn't want this one to be.

Knowing that my date was probably as uptight about me as I was about her, I figured what we needed was an icebreaker before our date even got started.

So I took a brown paper grocery bag and cut two holes in it for my eyes, and drew on a smile. On the forehead I wrote, "Your blind date for tonight," and drew an arrow pointing downward.

My plan was, if her imagination was getting the best of her—like mine was—she'd be expecting a really ugly guy. When she saw the paper bag, she'd wonder just how ugly I was if I had to walk around with a paper bag on my head.

That way, when I took off the bag, she'd be so relieved that I wasn't a nightmare that I'd look pretty good. I'm a normal-looking guy, but I'd probably look like a dream date after I took off the bag, right? We'd have a big laugh over it, we'd get over the nervous stage, and it would be smooth sailing from there. That was the plan.

It was drizzling, so I took an umbrella up to her door with me to protect her dress. I put on my paper bag, rang her doorbell, then, in a flash of creativity, I opened the umbrella and held it in front of my face so she couldn't see me.

The door opened, and a sweet, Southern voice said, "Oh ma *gosh*! Aren't you *cute* to bring an umbrella! Put it down so I can *see* you!"

I lowered my umbrella, smiling behind my bag, and thought I'd been hit by a stun gun. Marty was the largest woman I'd ever seen.

I had to look up to see her face, which was pretty, but she stood at least 6'6". Her pink frothy dress was supposed to have a belt, because I could see the belt loops, but she wasn't wearing one, probably because she couldn't get it around her waist. Marty's dress was one solid drop of pink ruffles from her huge shoulders down to her pink pumps. She looked like a pink slab with a head and two little pink feet. Her arms were twice as big around as mine. I'm a marathon runner, so I'm thin, and she was about four times as wide as I was, and seven inches taller.

I gulped. With my bagged head tilted up toward her face, her lips said, "Well, I'll be. If this isn't the funniest thing!"

I was glad I was wearing my bag so she wouldn't have seen the look of pure horror on my face, and I just hoped that the holes in the bag were off-center and had hidden the terror in my eyes.

She said, "Come on! *Take* your bag off. I know you're in there!"

I took it off, and Marty said, "Oh, ma God! What a surprise!"

Yes, it was a surprise all right. That bag had served a dual purpose after all: icebreaker and horror-hider.

Then her face clouded and she said, "That's not supposed to be a hint to me or anything now, is it?"

"Oh, no!" I said, crumpling it up. "Not at all. Just a little joke. Glad you liked it!"

It took her a little while to believe me and relax. But she must have gotten over it, because at the ball, she asked me to dance to every slow song. I would clutch at her belt loops, and I would almost pass out each time, because she'd step right on my feet with her high heels and stab my toes.

There was one dance I wanted to sit out, but Marty insisted. It was the dance where guys line up on one side, women on the other, and each person takes a turn dancing down the line. When her time came and she held one finger high over her head, lifted her skirt with the other hand, and danced and twirled her way down the line like a huge pink bowling ball, I figured she was having a good time after all, even if we'd both had a rocky start.

—Sean, 29, dentist, La Jolla

* * *

Spotting him across the bar, I knew I was in for a good beginning. He looked normal, reasonably attractive, and, from the way he was flirting with the waitress, friendly. This was one blind date that would work out. In fact, I'd make it work out. This was about as normal-looking and -sounding a date as I'd had in months.

We shook hands, smiled, I ordered a drink, and we smiled at each other some more.

He said, "So, tell me. I'm not clear on what you do for a living. What do you do?"

I settled back in my chair.

"Well, I review reading plans for the state. I make suggestions on which plans we might consider for future years, or which plans are unsuitable. There are some really interesting programs these days. For instance, today I read a brief on—"

He held up his hand to stop me, and said, "This isn't a job interview. Let's change the subject. Better yet, let's get a check. This isn't going to work out. Don't you agree? Tell you what, you go ahead and leave, and I'll settle up. Thanks for stopping by. Nice meeting you."

Actually, every job interview I'd ever been on had gone better than this split-second date. Was it something I said?

—Fran, 26, education department, South Carolina

* * *

Yikes, that was the smallest movie theater I'd ever seen. There were about ten rows of seats and about ten seats per row, and almost all were taken. My stomach always knotted in this movie situation; it was time to either split up or finagle two seats together.

I hunted for a possibility and found it: empty seat, man, woman, empty seat, and then a solid row of people. If the couple moved down a seat, my date, Barbara, and I could sit together.

It was our first date. Barbara said, "What are you waiting for? Do you want me to do it?"

I should have let her, but I felt that since I picked the movie, our seats were my responsibility.

I said, "No. You can fight for seats the next time."

I leaned over the empty aisle, smiled, and said, "Excuse me, is there any chance of my date and I sitting together?"

The couple looked at me, looked at each other, and continued their conversation.

I was embarrassed. The people in the row behind were tittering about my getting shot down.

I cleared my throat and said, "Excuse me. Would you mind if we took two seats together?"

The couple conferred, and glared at me with contempt.

The man said, "Be more specific. You're vague."

I heard Barbara sigh, and I said, "If the seats on either side of you are free, would you mind moving one seat one way or the other?"

I wanted to stay courteous.

The couple looked at each other, then at me.

The woman said, "What you're actually saying is that you'd like us to stand up and move to accommodate you."

Huh? What was I saying that wasn't getting through?

I said, "Yes, please. There are four seats. You take two together, and we'll take two together."

The man said, "We have our two together."

People were listening and giggling. Now I was getting mad. The only communication problem was getting two stingy people to give up the seats they were using as their coatrests. They were deliberately refusing me.

I said, "Let's put it this way. Move down."

The guy said, "You want us to move down so that you and your date can sit together."

I said, "Yes."

The man said, "You should have said so from the beginning instead of being ambiguous. You don't get anything in this world being obscure."

They moved down a seat, and my date and I sat down.

From several rows behind me, and to the right, I heard, "Hey, buddy, you want to get anywhere, you've got to be direct!"

I was getting smaller and smaller. Soon I'd be wearing knickers and asking for my mommy.

Barbara said, "Do something. Say something."

I said, "To whom? Who said that? Was it a man or a woman? Point for me."

She said, "You're letting them all walk all over you. Can't you hear everyone talking about it? It's so embarrassing."

I said, "Any minute now, the lights will go down and it'll be dark and everyone will forget about it. Relax."

Barbara said, "What a way to sit down to a movie. It hasn't even started and I'm ready to go."

I ignored that comment.

As we were all filing out after the movie, I had almost forgotten the confrontation until someone yelled, "Hey, buddy! Don't wimp out next time, man!"

Barbara yelled an obscenity to the unseen advice dispenser.

Outside, on the sidewalk, to add salt to the wound, she said, "You've got to learn to stick up for yourself."

I said, "You're right."

Her look of disdain said, "Gosh, you're a wimp," and she stormed off.

—Benjamin, 40, newspaper editor, Missouri

✳ ✳ ✳

Wat a crush I had on him. I was thirteen, he was four-teen. His locker was seven doors down from mine, and every time his eyes caught mine, I could feel myself blush, and I'd turn and disappear into the crowd.

How could he even know I was alive? He was older, on the football team, hung around with the "in" kids, and was active in every club in school. He was a star, and I was a regular student. If he ever so much as said hello to me, I knew I would just melt, and my dreams would have come true. That would be enough.

On Valentine's Day, I was exchanging little gifts with my best friend when someone tapped my shoulder.

It was him. And he was looking right at me! I couldn't look away and couldn't blink, and felt twisted up and hot and embarrassed and excited.

He held out a card to me and said, "This is for you."

I stared at him, and he pressed the card in my hand. My friend nudged me from behind, giggling, and I opened the card in a haze of surprised love.

I don't remember what the card said, other than it was romantic. What got my full attention was a little square of paper taped to the bottom right-hand corner.

I looked closer, mesmerized by this extra token of love. It said, "$2.99." I read it again. "$2.99."

He said, "Yeah. It set me back two dollars and ninety-nine cents because it's big and has one of those cellophane covers on it. Have you ever had a card this expensive?"

Before I could answer, he said, "Like my jacket? One hundred and sixty-five dollars. See these hiking boots? Eighty-five dollars. This shirt was sixty dollars. And these socks are cashmere, twenty dollars a pair. This diving watch cost two hundred and thirty-five dollars. That's a nice watch you've got on. What'd that cost?"

"It was on sale. I don't remember," I said. "Thanks. 'Bye."

That was not the last time my romantic crushes would instantly turn out to be duds, but it was the only time I ever had my hopes dashed by a cost-overrun inventory of everything on a guy's body.

—Shelby, 16, student, Vermont

* * *

told her that I couldn't ice skate, roller skate, rollerblade, snow ski, surfboard, skateboard, water-ski, or windsurf.

But there we were, at a frozen pond in Maine, and she was tying skates onto my feet, telling me that I'd be a natural. She wanted to spend the day ice skating.

I repeated the list of blade-, board-, and wheel-related activities that I couldn't do. She told me to stop being so modest, that no one was ever that much of a klutz.

She led me out to the ice with her arm around my waist. Gliding together in a straight line wasn't so bad. She was right.

She let go of me and I wobbled, but held my balance. I smiled at her, then took a header and slid about seven feet. Lying there, I was sure I had a concussion. I had felt this exact same way when I crashed when I went rollerblading.

She helped me get to my feet, and I immediately fell backwards, landing with a thud on my behind. I had a bruised tailbone. I recognized the symptoms from when I had a wipeout on a skateboard.

She helped me get up again, and I took another header. I was determined to keep smiling.

The thing is, the first time you fall, it's kind of cute. The second time you fall, that's cute, too. The third time you fall, that's okay. By the fifth or sixth fall, that's when they leave you on a bench and go off on their own.

I knew this, because it happened every time.

—David, 32, travel agent, Alabama

* * *

Snooze alarm. That's what this guy was. It was our first phone call, and he was boring me to tears. He was calling to set up our date. We'd met at the magazine section of a new megabookstore that was gaining a reputation for being a singles scene on weekend nights. I had planted myself near the collection of car and boat magazines—since my goal was to meet a guy, the fashion section was out of the question. He'd seemed okay, so we exchanged numbers.

He was putting me to sleep, so I pushed the phone to my ear with my shoulder, flipped through the papers in the "in" box on my desk, said, "Can you hang on for just a minute?" and hit the hold button on my phone.

I turned to Jeff, who had a desk nearby, and said, "Here I go again with another schmuck. I can't believe this. I can tell already that he's a total bore. Help me out here. How do I get out of this?"

Jeff opened his mouth, and a male voice said, "Don't bother. You already did."

Jeff's mouth hadn't moved. The voice had come from the phone.

I guess I hadn't hit the hold button after all, and my date had heard. My mouth fell open and the blood rushed to my face.

I gulped and said, "So, I guess we're not going out, are we?" I was really relieved, but so guilty that I felt like I had to go out with him as penance or I'd have to live with this horrible behavior of mine, this cruelty toward a prospective lousy date, for the rest of my life. I'm Catholic.

He said, "Well, do you want to get a bite to eat after work?"

Darn. What a creep. Couldn't he take a hint?

—Willa, 22, marketing, Detroit, Michigan

* * *

5

❋ ❋ ❋ ❋

Sex: Something Wild

Fetishes, compulsions, leanings. Passions, perversions, proclivities.
And we're just getting warmed up.

Last year, I worked at a bookstore where the manager was a Daniel Day-Lewis lookalike. I was infatuated the second I laid eyes on Chad. I was a sophomore in college. He was thirty-one.

Most of the employees would go out socially as a group, to the movies, to hear music, to someone's house for a dinner. But management's policy was that there be no romance whatsoever. No matter how I tried to orchestrate a situation where I could be alone with Chad for even five minutes, he'd always find someone to add to our duo. The management policy seemed to have Chad reined in.

Even so, after Christmas break, I took a deep breath and said, "Chad, why don't you come over tonight and have dinner with me?"

His sapphire eyes bored right into my brain and he said, "You know what you have in mind isn't appropriate."

I said, "I know. You're right. So go to a movie with me."

He looked at me in that sad-wise way he had that made me swoon, and said, "Please, no." I swooned some more at such a romantic, tragic-sounding rebuff. He was more terrific than I ever dreamed.

That Saturday night, I was sitting home with my roommate eating popcorn and watching a midnight movie, a campy old sci-fi adventure about a spaceship of aliens that crash-lands in a canyon. They captured a few humans and drugged them. They gave the woman drugs that made her hallucinate, then she tied a man with chains and beat him silly while the aliens took notes.

Right then, the phone rang. I answered. It was Chad's soft voice, saying my name.

"Yeah, yeah, it's me. Chad? Hi. Boy, it's late. What are you doing?" I pantomimed to my roommate with huge gestures, mouthing *Chad* to her twice. Her mouth flew open, and, still sitting, she bounced up and down on the sofa, clutching a pillow.

I caught a glimpse of myself in the mirror. I looked like someone was offering me a million dollars.

Chad said, "I'm watching a science fiction movie."

I said, "Me too! I can't believe this! This is great! Let me turn down the volume on my TV and see if I can hear yours over the phone!"

I stood up, then covered the mouthpiece and said to my roommate, "I can't believe I said that. That was so stupid. I lose my mind around him."

Chad said, "Come over."

I cleared my throat and said, "Sure. When? Lunchtime?"

Chad, sounding sexy, said, "No. Now."

"Now?" I looked in the mirror. No, I needed at least an hour to look like a humanoid. I'd been painting the kitchen all day and needed to take another shower. I'd have to shave my legs, wash my hair, blow it dry. . . . Why tonight, of all nights? I looked at the clock, feeling cunning. "I'll come by

when the show's over," I said, knowing I could do everything I needed to do and drive over within thirty minutes
if I rushed.

Chad said, "Now is better for me. I know you're interested
in me, and I'm interested in you. We just won't tell management. The only thing is, I'm a submissive."

I motioned to my roommate to turn down the TV.

"You're a what?" I asked, not being at all familiar with that
particular religion, but ready to convert.

"I'm looking for a dominatrix," Chad said matter-of-factly.
"Some experience doesn't hurt, but a quick study could fill the
bill."

I said, "A dominatrix? What would that entail?" I felt like
I was at a job interview. Next he'd probably specify part-time
or full-time.

Chad said, "You would tie me up, then you'd beat me with
a natural-bristle hairbrush I brought back from England. You'd
ride me around the room, whipping me with a flyswatter."

I said, "Hm. Is this the only way we can have a relationship?" I was still hopeful.

Chad said it was.

I said, "How long would I have to perform those duties before things went more conventionally?"

Chad said, "Take it or leave it."

I said I was flattered by the offer, but would have to pass
at this time. "By the way," I said, "what brought this on? I've
been after you for months."

Chad said, "It was the movie. That chain scene was a real
scorcher."

I said, "Chad, before you hang up, just one thing. I'll do
the dominatrix thing at work, though. That might be fun. We'd
both like that. Like, if you tell me to stock the shelves, I'll say,
'No, do it yourself.' "

Chad said, "I'll say, 'You're fired.' "

I said, "I don't know what happened. You just went

dominatrix on me. You're complicated, Chad. See you Monday. Good luck tonight."

—Olivia, 20, student, Honolulu

* * *

Making love—that's what we would've been doing in less than five seconds. Countdown! Off with the last piece of her clothing. Liftoff!

She murmured in my ear, "Tell me what you like."

I told her, thrilled to be asked, especially by someone I was going to bed with for the first time. What a bonanza.

I waited for her to act on my information.

She said, "Do you want to know what I like?"

Well, I did, but I thought we'd have that discussion after we got through Act I.

I said, "Sure."

She said, "First, I like to be kissed here." She pointed.

"Then," she said, "you can kiss me here. Then I like to have my back kissed. You can also give me a light mini–back massage, Shiatsu style, not Swedish. Then I like to have the insides of my arms caressed, at the crease, right here. I also like to have my ears nibbled, and the nape of my neck massaged. When you're through with that . . ."

That must be about the time I felt myself nodding off.

We were both dates from hell.

—Peter, 30, chiropractor, Oklahoma City

* * *

"Let's experiment," I blurted out to my boyfriend. We were in bed, making love, and after ten years of going out, we'd gotten a little stale in the passion department.

He looked quizzical, then said, "Really?"

I said, "Uh-huh. Why not? We're legal, consenting adults."

He scratched his head and said, "Okay. Like what?"

I wasn't sure. I hadn't thought that far ahead.

I decided to start with traditional kinky.

I said, "Tie me up."

It was like a klieg light hit his face. He brightened, jumped off the bed, and disappeared. In one minute, he was back, using one hand to gather my wrists and hold them straight up, the other to grab my ankles and lift them straight over my chest. In a blur of movement, he stepped back and loudly said, "Done!" looking ecstatic.

I had asked for it, all right.

My boyfriend was a cowboy. He worked the cattle on a ranch, and he had just hog-tied me—apparently in record-time—like he would a calf. My wrists were tied to my ankles. I could tell you this much, he was good at it. I could wiggle my toes and fingers, but other than that, I couldn't move. I was formed into a triangle.

My boyfriend was giving his handiwork a good looking-over. He pursed his lips into a "not bad" expression.

"Honey," I said matter-of-factly, "you did get a great job."

"Well, thank you. What now?" he asked, scratching his head but looking interested, like maybe he should heat up the branding iron, or feed me some hay.

"Untie me, and bring me some juice," I said.

"Want to watch a little Letterman?" he asked, loosening the rope.

Sounded good to me.

—Gwynn, 36, pilot, San Antonio

* * *

"You're kidding, right?" I asked, staring down at him. What had happened to my date? Who was this lunatic?

After a nice, formal dinner that his company threw, we went to his house for a drink. He was a senior vice president, had a nice house, midpriced car, good manners. It was our second date, and I was thrilled to be out with someone regular rather than the quirky, self-consumed types I was usually attracted to.

He poured brandy and handed me his family album to look at. Then he'd dropped to the floor, resting his head on my lap. That was nice. Sweet, cozy, and nice.

Then he took my high heels off my feet, which felt great, and started massaging the soles of my feet.

He said, "Does that feel good?"

I said, "Yes," and he said, "Good. Do mine!"

He hopped onto the couch, yanked off his socks and shoes, and said, "Do it like this. Here's what I want. Suck on my toes, big toe first, then work your way down to the little toes, okay?"

I looked straight ahead, trying to comprehend, and coming into focus were four or five baby pictures on the mantel—of him.

He repeated, "I like my little toes best, don't you?"

I stood up, said I'd call a cab, and thought to myself, *I sure can pick 'em.*

—Valerie, 27, software analyst, Memphis

✳ ✳ ✳

Steaks sounded good to me!

My date was making us dinner. He said he was preparing a barbecue for two. It was our eighth date, and we still hadn't done much more than kiss, which didn't bother me. When and if the time was right, it'd happen. I liked that he wasn't rushing or pushing, that we were having a textbook case of a normal, healthy relationship.

He put the platter of raw steaks on the coffee table and sat beside me on the couch.

"I'll season these while we talk," he said.

I felt rosy and warm. It was such a cozy moment.

Then he took off his shirt and laid down on the couch, scooting his legs behind me.

He was feeling amorous. So was I!

He reached for the steaks, put one on each side of his chest, and said, "Can you lick my ankles while I flip these?"

So much for the cozy feeling. I stood up and grabbed my purse, but couldn't resist flipping his steaks for him. Then I left.

—Rachel, 22, pharmacist, Nebraska

✳ ✳ ✳

Indirect lighting, top-of-the-line stereo speakers, bouncy new carpet. Heck, my apartment didn't look that good, and that was just her closet. She had one of those old-timey closets the size of a living room.

"Well, I'll be," I said, seeing that there was a picnic table inside.

She faced me, then pushed me backwards against the picnic table. I thought we should swap positions, but, truth is, I didn't want splinters in my behind or my knees, so I said, "I'd rather have rug burns than splinters. How about you? How's the floor look to you?"

Right then my watch caught in her hair, and I said, "Sorry."

She reached to one of the shelves, opened up a switchblade, took my wrist, and sliced off the band of my watch. Then, smiling seductively, she sliced the button off the waistband of my jeans.

Maybe I overreacted. All I know is, I said, "I'm outta here. I can't stay for the rest of this show," and dove into my truck and drove off.

—Tom, 31, surveyor, New Hampshire

✳ ✳ ✳

After our third date, we went back to his place for a nightcap.

He led me to the bedroom, turned off the lights, and pulled me onto the bed.

Then he reached to his nightstand, handed me something, and said, "Would you mind?"

Mind? This was the nineties, and I was thrilled that he was conscientious and practiced safe sex.

"Not at all," I said, reaching through the darkness to find his hand.

I was latching onto something hard.

He flipped on the bedside lamp and said, "Would you? I'd like it."

I was holding a book of lullabies.

"Read me the first one," he said, putting his hands under his head, looking excited.

I turned the book over in my hands, then flipped through it, looking for the kinky parts he'd probably slipped in. But it was a basic bedside book for kids.

I said, "You're serious?"

He said, "Yeah. It's exciting. Just one, that's all. And I'll take off my tie for you."

I sighed, sat beside him, and said, "What the heck. Once upon a time . . ."

When I was through, his eyes were bright. He took off his necktie and said, "Read me one more, and I'll take off my shirt."

Granted, it was a weird situation, but I felt safe, and I was curious. I had never known anyone to get revved by bedtime stories.

I was surprised that I had read the second story so fast. I was getting into the swing of it, so I wasn't upset when he said, "Read me another one and I'll take off my belt."

Believe it or not, I did. I didn't have any nieces or nephews, and so hadn't had any reason to drop back to childhood books before. I was enjoying this.

"Have you read *A Wrinkle in Time*?" I asked. "That was always one of my favorites."

He shook his head, lifting his hips to slide his belt through the back loops.

"Keep reading," he said, and tugged on his shirt, cueing me to the next piece of clothing that would come off.

I was sitting on the edge of the bed, more like a nanny than a lover.

I took stock of the situation. Pants, two shoes, two socks. I was looking at three more stories minimum, five maximum.

I wasn't in the groove for reading aloud anymore, and certainly not in the mood for more kiddie stories. It was clear that he wouldn't be in the groove for adult pursuits until I'd put a dent in the storybook.

He tugged some more at his shirt, lifted his eyebrows, and said, "Read me the first one again."

I said, "No. I'll read this other one. Here goes."

I read the first paragraph and the last, and when he said, "Hey, you skipped the middle," I said, "No, I skipped the whole night. Sweet dreams."

I turned off the light, and as I let myself out of his apartment, I heard him snoring lightly.

—Samantha, 35, veterinarian, Indianapolis

✳ ✳ ✳

6

✳ ✳ ✳ ✳

Chain Reactions

You have absolutely zero control over gravity, time, or fate. What's going on? One catastrophe after another keeps hurling toward you. Talk about relentless. What can you do to handle it? *Duck!*

Who could have guessed they'd start ganging up on her? We were on a blind date, at a comedy club. Her name was Nancy, she was a radiologist, and though she wasn't great-looking, it didn't scare me to look at her. The best thing about her was that she had this sweet side, and a vulnerability that made me feel a little protective—maybe it was the wispy blond hair and big blue eyes.

Anyway, we'd had a pleasant enough dinner, no fireworks in the chemistry department or anything, but nothing crippling (like my most recent chain of blind dates), and so we went on to the comedy club.

The place was jammed. We were meeting our two-drinks-per-person-per-set minimum with ease—me with beer, her with ginger ale. We'd had our quota (I had no idea drinks were $8 each) before the show began. Then the room went black, and with a great fanfare of an introduction, there he was, the first comic. And that's when it started.

He opened with, "Hey, anyone from out of town?"

And suddenly someone yelled, "Hey, that's original!"

I looked around to see who'd said it, but couldn't tell.

The comic ignored the heckle and said, "Thank you very much. Moving right along, has this ever happened to you? You do your wash, and later, when you're matching the socks, one's missing, and you know that's the one that made a break for it and—"

"Yeah! Like no one watches Seinfeld! Next!"

My mouth fell open. It was Nancy. My date was sitting in the dark, perched tensely on the edge of her seat, with a slightly mean look on her pixie features, cracking a piece of ice in half, watching the comic with an intensity I'd never seen before. Like a tiger waiting confidently for the next chance to take a swipe at the little baby deer with a big paw of claws.

The comic put his hand over his eyes like a scout, peering into the darkness, and said, "Mom! Is that you? She's still trying to convince me to get a day job. Anyway, where was I . . ."

He only did a few more minutes, ending fast, to lukewarm clapping. He also ended it by peering intently into the audience at the end, like he was trying to divine who'd thrown him off stride. No luck. His eyes skimmed right over sweet-looking Nancy, probably homing in on some innocent biker chick in the back.

The lights came up, and I said, "Uh, Nancy. What was that about?"

She popped two sticks of gum in her mouth, offered me one, and said, "What? Sh. Here's the next one."

This comic seemed to gingerly take the stage, looking carefully at each face in the front row.

"HOW YA DOIN'?" he bellowed, jarring the room. "I hear you're a tough audience. Love's tough. Right? How 'bout you two?" He pointed to a couple in the front row. "You think love's tough?"

A voice yelled, "No, but this crummy act is!"

"Pardon me for living. What we got in the house today? A

couple of yutes—I said yutes—shaking things up? I come from New York. That's what's great about New York, right? Yutes. What the heck is that? Yutes. I'll give you an example—"

The voice interrupted, "Don't bother. We saw *My Cousin Vinny*, and Joe Pesci does it better."

That was all Nancy did to this one. He mumbled, "How 'bout dat? I had a whole Joe Pesci act, and it's au revoir to that riff. Who's out there? Marisa Tomei?" He wound it up fast.

There was a big pause before the next comic came on. I used that time to say, "I hope you don't take offense to this or anything, but I don't think it's a great idea to talk to the comic."

Nancy squinted her eyes, crunched her ice, and said, "They love it. It's like interactive TV. They live for give-and-take. Loosen up."

I checked for a path to the door, but there was no such thing. They'd crammed tables together, and it was so smoky I couldn't see the door. The third victim was taking the stage.

He started up with, "Hey blondie, got anything to say? Say it now or forever hold your peace. Say something so I can work around you. You want to take the stage? Come on up here. Please. Be my guest."

Nancy's eyes lit up. He was talking to her, all right. I rubbed my right eye, which was throbbing. Oh, no. Things were coming unglued. I leaned my body away from Nancy, trying to look like I was with the table next to ours. Maybe she'd hush up and let the night crawl by till we could make a run for it. She was silent.

"THANK you," the comic barked, huffing and puffing a little for dramatic effect. "So, I flew in today—on a plane. They ought to rename the coach section SRO—standing room only. It's like Calcutta these days."

Oh no. Another lame beginning. We could all smell blood, so it was not too traumatic when Nancy yelled, "What's with those oxygen masks and the stewardess hand motions and that red curtain that separates first class? Wow."

A man said, "Zip it up, lady."

A woman behind us said, "Leave him alone."

The comic said something obscene about what he'd like to do with the microphone, which made a couple of people in the audience hiss.

He was quick, too. When he rapidly left the stage, I put my face in my hands.

The fourth one said, "Hello, don't hurt me. I'm sensitive. Like I told my therapist—"

"Can your therapist stay awake?" Nancy yelled.

"I get a free session for every referral," the comic said, "and you look like a free pass to me."

"When's the last time you had any luck making a pass?" Nancy said.

I eyed the floor. I could crawl out, between feet and table legs. That was looking easy compared to staying where I was.

The fifth comic began with, "Lady, your date looks mortified. The people sitting around you look mortified. Everyone backstage wants to strangle your neck. Tell us one good thing about your life."

Nancy thought for a minute, which only I and the audience knew was dangerous, and just as the comic relaxed, she said, "I'm not a humorless comic subjecting an audience to my anger."

"No, you're a humorless *person* subjecting comics to your anger," the comic said, looking angry. "Let me guess. You're on a blind date, right? What was my first clue? I'm psychic. Some of the people you work with don't talk to you? I'm cooking now. Forget the act. Let's talk about you some more."

Nancy's face went blank. Word must have been spreading backstage, all right. Now they were scrapping their acts, coming out with the intent of gunning for Nancy.

I whispered, "Let's leave. Get your bag. Let's go."

She was in a trance.

The next comic, a woman, started with, "I have a younger sister just like you. You're the youngest, right? Whine, whine,

whine. Are you even on speaking terms with anyone in your family? Of course, being the youngest myself, I know how it is. And the youngest child is the gifted child. But you're a real pain in the ass in general, aren't you? How's that blind date going? Think you'll get a kiss out of this one? I DOUBT it, don't you?"

Nancy rallied and said, "At least I'm on a date," and someone in the audience said, "Give it a rest."

The comic said, "Think you'll hear from your date again? Let's ask him."

I wanted to sink through the floor. I was feeling clammy. I was no hero. I was just a guy on another date that wasn't going well, I wanted to say into a microphone.

Nancy jumped to her feet and somehow managed to push her way out of the club. The audience began applauding. As Nancy disappeared, the previous comics came on stage, clapping, and the audience got to its feet, delivering a standing ovation. I stayed in my chair, accidentally swallowing my gum.

The next two comics ran through their sets, but the adrenaline rush had distracted the audience, which was now surprised and jubilant and energized by their ovation. There was a constant low hum of murmuring. How had things gotten this out of hand?

Only one more comic to go, and a small chorus of boos started up.

Nancy, head held high, was winding her way back to the table. I felt the room tilt—I was in a bad dream. The boos started up in the audience, and the last comic came on stage, booing. Out came the other comics, booing.

The last comic yelled, "Come on, ladies and gentlemen! Work the last set with me! Boooo!"

The audience was on its feet again, booing, as Nancy and I zigzagged through the crowd and barreled out the door.

Nancy's eyes were red. She looked stunned. I felt cheated, and it had nothing to do with her. I was the only one who hadn't participated all night, not heckling a comic like Nancy had, nor heckling Nancy like the comics and the audience had. Even at football games, I was the only one who stayed seated for the Wave.

I had an urge to needle her, say, "Way to go," but instead I drove her home. I waited until she'd gotten out of the car. Then, heading home, I tried out a couple of "yutes," felt the tension start to leave my body, and made myself two promises. One, next time I was in a Wave, I'd be a player. And two, next time a date hassled a performer, I'd run for the nearest fire exit. Participation had its limits.

—Kurt, 28, actor, Los Angeles

✳ ✳ ✳

Gabrielle would walk forty-eight states, and through fire, to get a date. For her, no effort was too much when it came to dating. On the other hand, I hated useless dating conversation, especially the first couple of conversations. They were painfully boring and ridiculous. For instance, did I really care if someone I didn't know got into graduate school, if he should have taken more prep courses for his GREs? No.

That was why I made my older sister Gabrielle do that disgusting part for me. We sounded identical on the phone. We looked similar, too, except that she was 5'3" and I was 5'6". Gabrielle didn't mind, actually. She regarded it as practice for her own dating conversations. She had enough dates, but guys weren't usually as interested in her as they were in me. I was sure it was because she looked so earnest, and they mistook my boredom for mystery or something equally juvenile.

When I met Michael at a party, I cued Gabrielle that he'd be calling. On a Tuesday night, the phone rang, and leaving a message on our answering machine was Michael. Gabrielle picked up, and chirped, "Hi! What a nice surprise! What's up? ... Well, thanks! I thought you were cute, too! ... You're kidding! You did? How fun! So, do you play softball *every*

Saturday afternoon? ... A home run? Good for you! I'm impressed!"

Gabrielle curled up on a big chair, chatting and charming away, giving me a thumbs-up. I breathed a sigh of relief. My first dating conversation with Michael was going like a dream. Later, I told Gabrielle what my end of the conversation would have sounded like: "Hi.... Thanks.... So? ... Huh."

Over the next two weeks, Gabrielle conducted my part of the phone conversation, filling me on the high points I'd need to know if the guy ever got around to asking me out.

I said, "What's he waiting for? What a jerk."

"He's just really uptight about his job. He has a new boss who's making him work weekends, too, and he's under a lot of pressure. Plus, a guy at his office is trying to get promoted over him, so he's at wit's end. Don't be so hard on him. He's swamped."

I made a face and said, "Even in a political coup, there's time for a date." My sister was such a softie.

Finally, date night. Gabrielle was excited, I was mellow.

Dinner was stiff. He talked endlessly about his job, which I had already heard about in too much detail from Gabrielle, and I thought she told it better.

I didn't talk much. The thing was, I got tongue-tied when I was around a new guy. I just sort of clammed up and went into a nervous paralysis. That was the other reason, I guess I ought to have confessed, that I enlisted Gabrielle's help.

Toward the end of dinner, Michael said, "Am I boring you? You're so quiet. It's like I'm out with a different person than I've been talking to on the phone."

I gave him a big smile, praying that I wasn't giving him a lopsided sneer, and said, "Really? Uh, so, you play softball, right? I love softball. Tell me more about it."

He called the next day to see why I'd been so quiet, and Gabrielle said, "I wasn't feeling well, but I wanted to see you so much that I went anyway. Gosh, I hope I didn't ruin your evening. I feel so bad! Can you forgive me? Can we try again?

And I think I was nervous because I was so used to talking to you on the phone that I clammed up when there you were, sitting across from me at dinner. It was so weird! . . . Yeah? You felt the same way? . . . . Friday night is great! . . . I promise! Yes! I'll talk! You're so funny!"

Gabrielle hung up and firmly said to me, "You're on. Now don't blow it this time. I told you what to talk about. This one doesn't have the stamina to get to the fifth or sixth date when you start speaking. He's kind of vulnerable. You should be sensitive to that."

I said, "Hey! He's my date, not yours. I know when he's sensitive. You know, *I'm* the one who likes this guy."

The second date was almost as bad as the first, though I did say, "I'm so much more comfortable with you!" and Michael looked at me like I was from Mars and said, "Really? This went well for you? Okay . . ."

On our third date, Michael was starting to look downright sullen, and I was loosening up, wanting to know how his plan to hold off the worm at work was going.

Gabrielle was still having one-hour phone conversations with him, and she said that she had him in the palm of my hand.

On our fourth date, Michael spent most of the time staring intently, and quizzing me on our phone calls. I passed with flying colors. There was no way I couldn't, considering our phone was in the living room, and I had to listen to Gabrielle's end of the long-winded conversations every time he called.

I went home that night and told Gabrielle, "We kissed! It was great! I really like him! You have to do a few more phone calls, then I can take it from there."

Usually, Gabrielle said, "Great. It's about time."

This time, she said, "That's okay. I don't mind. I should probably keep handling the calls till you're one hundred percent sure."

I said, "No way. I'm the one who's dating him in the flesh, not you."

She glared at me. The phone rang, and I answered. It was Michael.

I said, "Yes, it's me. I had fun tonight," and smiled happily at Gabrielle.

Michael said, "Thanks, I'm glad. And I finally had the time to do some homework, and found out that you have a sister. Can I talk to Gabrielle for a second, then talk to you? I just got some bad news about my family, and I need to talk to her for some reason."

I handed Gabrielle the phone, and said, "He asked for you by name."

Her face lit up, and she started cooing, "I'm so sorry . . . you poor thing . . . stay there. I'll be right over."

I knew it was time to scrap this operation. It had started to backfire.

—Danielle, 22, lab technician, Kentucky

✳ ✳ ✳

Free tickets to the opera! My friend and her husband couldn't attend, and asked if I wanted their two tickets. The opera was for Saturday night, three nights away.

I already had a date booked that night with Phil. It would be our second date. We'd met on a bicycling excursion to the country, and we'd had one other date, attending a Schwarzenegger movie. I had no idea if opera was his cup of tea.

I called, told him it was also a dress-up, gala night with formal attire, and he said, "I'm game. Let's do it. Can't beat the price!"

I bought a black velvet dress that had sheer sleeves and was scooped low in the back, and I thought I looked great.

Phil, who had a car, said he would swing by my apartment to pick me up. My buzzer rang, and he announced himself and said his car was double-parked. I said I'd be right down.

As I got in the car, I waited for Phil to say something about my outfit. Instead, he said, "I almost got a ticket! While I was buzzing you, a parking cop was about to write a ticket! I couldn't believe it!"

I couldn't believe it either, and I was busy commiserating with him, so it was about a mile later when I noticed his clothes.

I said, "Phil, this is a formal night. I told you that, right?"

He was wearing a striped shirt, jeans, and a brown sports jacket.

He said, "Yeah, you told me. But I wanted to be comfortable. These operas can be really long."

I bit my tongue, but the words came out anyway. I said, "You're dressed for an afternoon baseball game."

Phil snickered, then snapped, "Look, opera isn't my thing. At least I'm going with you."

I said, "I had no idea this was a chore for you. I wish you'd said so. I could have asked someone else to go."

Phil shook his head and said, "I didn't mean it that way. I'm just uptight after that fight I had with the traffic cop. I'm happy I'm going, okay? I look all right. You'll see."

I let the subject drop, not wanting to get into a fight, even if he looked like a bum on our first romantic night out.

So I said, "You're wearing sneakers to the opera?"

I felt like I would hyperventilate.

Phil shot me a dirty look and said, "Do you want to argue? I've got my hands full with this traffic. Everyone's trying to cut in front of me. Hey, you jerk—get out of my way! I hate driving in the city. It makes me crazy."

I wanted to ask why we didn't take a taxi, but that was guaranteed to blossom into a full-fledged quarrel.

Traffic was rerouted due to construction, and we sat in silence for fifteen minutes while we didn't move an inch.

At last we were only a few blocks from Lincoln Center, with ten minutes until curtain time.

I said, "Let's splurge and park in the garage. It'll be faster."

Phil refused, saying that garage prices were obscene. I told him that the garage would be my treat, and he said, "No way. Those valet guys drive like maniacs. I'll find a space on the street. I always do."

We circled Lincoln Center once. As we completed the second swing around it, I couldn't suppress myself anymore and blurted out, "Let's just park in the garage. This is crazy. We're going to miss the beginning."

We were arguing, and starting our third crawl around the block, when Phil slammed on the brakes and exclaimed, "We're in luck! There's a space!"

He threw the car in reverse, eyed the rearview mirror, and proceeded to back up—and kept backing up.

I yelled, "What are you doing? We're going to get in an accident like this!"

Phil said, "Pipe down! I'm trying to concentra—"

That's when we heard and felt the impact of a crash.

Phil had somehow backed right into a Mercedes.

I said, "Don't most people turn their head around when they're backing up?"

Phil glared at me and said, "Maybe if you hadn't been complaining the whole time I wouldn't have been distracted."

The Mercedes driver told Phil to pull into the space, they exchanged information, and Phil and I ran to Lincoln Center.

Even though he was in sneakers and I was in heels, I was twenty feet ahead of him as I raced into the lobby.

An usher stopped me and said, "I'm sorry. The performance began thirty minutes ago. You can't go in until intermission."

I gasped and said, "When's intermission?"

The usher looked at his watch and said, "In forty-five minutes. You can watch on closed-circuit TV, however."

Phil and I sat on a banquette, looking at the opera on the tiny screen, while we both fumed, furious with each other.

We didn't say a word for a while, then I broke the ice with, "This is great," I said. "Hunting for a space and having a wreck saved so much money that we're sitting in the lobby watching the opera on TV."

Phil said, "Maybe we would have been here sooner if you'd been helping me find a space instead of ragging on me."

We bickered on the banquette for ten minutes before we noticed that we were disturbing everyone around us. We stood up and decided to go across the street for a drink until intermission, and to double-check on our dinner reservations.

At the restaurant, the maître d' told us he didn't have a clue who we were.

I said, "Phil, you said you called."

Phil said, "You said you'd make the reservation."

We sat at the bar and had a drink.

Neither of us was hungry, and we both were uncomfortable with each other, still upset.

After the drink, I said, "Well, should we call it a night?"

He nodded. Neither of us was in the mood to concentrate on a performance, and we weren't thrilled about being in each other's company. What was the point of going back after intermission?

I said I'd grab a taxi, but Phil insisted on driving me home, and I agreed.

When we got to my apartment building, we shook hands.

I said, "I'm sorry it turned out so bad."

Phil said, "Me, too. Sometimes it happens, I guess."

Halfheartedly, I said, "Maybe we should try something different next time."

Phil agreed, said he would call, and I went upstairs.

I never heard from him again, and I was glad. If he had called, I had no idea if I wanted to see him again. The problem wasn't just that everything had gone wrong, or that we had squabbled, but that we had argued as openly as a couple does when they're years into a relationship. We had skipped any courtship stage of pretending that neither of us had any irritations that weren't cute.

Arguing like an old married couple can really stall out a second date.

—Mae, 41, interior designer, Brooklyn

* * *

'd met Barbara at a bar the week before, and had called to ask her for a date. She said she and her girlfriends were going to a Halloween party Saturday night, and I could join them if I dressed up in a costume. It sounded like fun, so I agreed.

They picked me up, and I loved the goose bumps I got. Barbara was dressed like Morticia, another friend was a dead ringer for Gomez, and the third like Wednesday from *The Addams Family*. They were upset that I hadn't dressed up—all I'd brought was a Richard Nixon mask that I wore every year.

Barbara was driving. The plan was to party-hop; they knew of three. The first party was a dud, mainly because we were too early. On the way to the second party, which was clear across town, the one dressed like Wednesday started to moan. Her moans got louder as we drove. She clutched her stomach, practically screaming. We all panicked and agreed that we should head to an emergency room.

We were going right by my apartment, and I asked if they'd let me out. Barbara snapped, "I can't believe you said that. Some support you turn out to be," and flew by my house.

I was the first one to hear the sirens. Barbara didn't slow down, even when the glare of flashing red lights was swishing through the car.

"Pull over!" I kept yelling, while Barbara told me to mind my own business.

The police blasted over their speaker, "Pull over immediately." She did.

One policeman came up to the car cautiously, and did a double take when Morticia faced him. He peered in to see

Gomez, and the groaning Wednesday in the seat next to Richard Nixon.

"Step out of the car, miss," he said.

While Barbara, muttering, did as she was told, I pushed back my mask and said, "Officer, it's sort of an emergency. And I told her to pull over, but she didn't hear your siren. Plus—"

Barbara cut me off, pointing over her shoulder to me and saying, "He's just along for the ride. What's the problem, anyway? Low blood sugar? Don't feel like going after anyone who isn't in costume?"

I gasped, a jail cell flashing before my eyes, and got out of the car. I saw the second officer shining a flashlight in the back seat.

"Officer, she's right," I said. "I'm just some guy who picked her up at a bar last week and agreed to go out with all of them tonight—not to date all of them, but when I asked her out, she said I could tag along to their parties. I've never seen these other two before. Maybe I should just get going."

The officer said, "Get back in the car. Tell the one who's making the noise to step out."

I scrambled back into the car, pushing out Wednesday.

The officer took one look at Wednesday's contorted face and said, "Looks like appendicitis. Get back in the car, all of you, and follow us."

Barbara revved the engine, glared in the rearview mirror, and said, "Thanks a million. You're such a gentleman. What was that stuff about just trying to cut out on us? You're pathetic."

I got some digs of my own in, feeling sheepish about how nasty and low things had gotten, but, frankly, I didn't know those people, and the night had gotten too weird. Wednesday was groaning, and the other girl was screaming at Barbara to keep up with the police car, while Barbara was screaming back at her.

At the hospital, we all raced in while Barbara parked the

car and joined us in the emergency room, where everyone except Wednesday was reading magazines.

We were an odd group, but we fit in somehow, with the crowd assembled at eleven at night. Barbara made two scenes with a nurse about making Wednesday wait, which probably bumped Wednesday further down the line.

Suddenly a gang burst into the emergency room, holding up a guy who was bleeding. They were agitated, speaking rapid-fire Spanish to the nurse. The nurse kept saying, "Inglés, inglés!" while the guy was bleeding like crazy. She yelled, "Does anyone here speak Spanish?"

We all looked around at each other. No one spoke up. Finally, taking a deep breath, I said, "I do."

The victim told me that he'd been stabbed in the stomach with a knife. Staring at the blood oozing down his shirt and pants, I felt green around the gills.

The nurse said, "Okay. You come with him and me." Oh no. She was talking to me. I glanced back at Barbara and her crew, who were staring at me. Yes, we were getting separated, and the Addams family group had started to look good to me.

Well, I was with Jorge for about four hours. He was a nice guy. In fact, we've had lunch twice since.

When I finally was allowed to say goodbye and go back into the waiting room, I glanced in the mirror and saw that I was covered in blood from Jorge. There were Barbara and Gomez. Barbara lifted her head and turned to face away from me. Her friend shot me a mean look and lifted a magazine to her nose.

I went outside and flagged a cab to take me home. I threw away my clothes. Barbara never called me, I never called her, and no matter how good my friends said that the movie *Addams Family Values* was, I never went near anything having to do with Morticia again.

—Dominic, 26, tennis pro, Mississippi

✳ ✳ ✳

S pending a long weekend on a sailboat sounded glorious, especially since I'd never had the chance before.

Matthew invited me. We met at a party and had two good dates. So when he showed me the photo of his boat and told me our mutual friend Paul would be coming, I accepted. We wouldn't be alone on a boat all weekend, and we'd have a friend along.

Friday afternoon we boarded at a Newport dock for the trip to Cape Cod. Aside from me, Matthew, and Paul, there was Paul's girlfriend Stacey, Paul's sister Polly, and Polly's friend Jane.

I was glad that the split was two guys and four women, because the living quarters were tight, allowing almost zero privacy. Since it was my first time on a sailboat, I was as nervous as I was happy.

That first night, with clear skies, bright stars, and chilly breezes, was like a fantasy. Long after everyone else went to sleep, Matthew and I stayed on deck, drinking a bottle of wine and kissing. It was the best date I'd ever had.

The next afternoon, we docked at the Cape. All of us except for Stacey, who was seasick, went ashore.

After dinner, we went to a small club that had dancing. We'd all had too much to drink. Matthew and I had been kissing in front of everyone, and we were oblivious.

After a great slow dance with him, I sat down and chatted with Paul. A fellow I didn't know asked me to dance. I didn't see Matthew, and Paul said, "Go ahead!"

The dance was fun, to "Mustang Sally," and when I sat down, I saw Matthew take the dance floor to a Rolling Stones tune with Polly. When the song ended, they danced two more times, then sat together at our table, whispering and laughing.

They were just friends.

When another guy I'd never seen before asked me to dance and I saw that Matthew didn't notice, I accepted, danced, and sat down again, watching Matthew whisper into Polly's ear as she collapsed in a gale of laughter.

I wondered what Paul was making of all this. Maybe he could tell me if I should be worried about my date and his sister. But Paul was on the dance floor, with his face buried in Jane's neck as they barely moved during a slow dance.

Everyone was getting rearranged. I couldn't believe it.

I danced two more times with the first guy who'd asked me, then tapped Matthew on the shoulder and said, "Dance with me," trying not to sound wounded.

I tapped once more before it was clear that he was so wrapped up in Polly that he didn't feel my taps or hear my voice.

Abruptly he stood up, forcing me to step back as he grabbed Polly's hand and led her to the dance floor.

I sat and simmered. I was jealous and mad. Polly was 5'8", weighed about 120 pounds, had blond hair down to her waist and big green eyes, and was a professional ballet dancer. She was uninhibited about dancing her heart out, catching the admiring stares of every guy in the joint.

I felt like a slug curled up in its shell, and refused other offers to dance. I wanted to dance with my date. Was that asking too much?

At closing time, we filed out. Paul said something to Matthew, and Matthew took my elbow and said, "Isn't that a great club? I *love* it! I love this night! I love all of you guys!"

I relaxed as his arm loped across my shoulders. I had been crazy to worry. Matthew was just feeling exuberant. I hoped no one except Paul had noticed how I'd been feeling.

We caught two taxis to the sailboat, taking a dinghy to get on board.

I stayed on deck, waiting for Matthew to join me, but he didn't.

I went down to the sleeping area, where we each had our bunk, even if they were beside or on top of one another.

Sardined onto one slab of a bed were Matthew and Polly, giggling and squirming.

I wanted to scream, but couldn't. Like a good scout, I

climbed onto my bunk, directly below theirs, and plotted murder. Once, when one of their feet banged my head, I said, "Watch it!" preparing for battle, but they giggled. I didn't sleep.

In the morning, we set out on a bike ride. Paul was riding alongside Jane more than he was his girlfriend Stacey. Needing a shoulder, I sought out the one person in the same situation I was in. I pedaled up beside Stacey and said, "Everything okay? You seem quiet."

I waited for a clouded face, but Stacey flashed me a gorgeous smile and said, "I feel great! Compared to last night, at least! I still feel queasy. I'm so glad that Paul and Jane are getting to be friends. It means I don't have to talk much. Isn't it a nice day?"

I said, "Do you think I should catch a ride back to Newport? Matthew and Polly shared a bunk last night. I feel like I shouldn't be here."

Stacey put her face up to the sun and said, "Matthew was in his own bunk this morning. They were drunk, and Matthew's a big flirt, is all. Relax."

I realized that I was talking to someone who was a bigger fool than I was. Up ahead, Matthew and Polly were holding hands while they rode abreast, then dropping hands to race. I felt sick.

We all went back to the boat, cast off, and spread our dinner fixings. I regretted not leaving the group. Now that we were at sail, it was clear that Matthew wasn't sure what my name was. Once he looked at me and said, "Uh ... Mary! Next time you get a beer, will you get one for me?"

I did, just so I could say, "Matthew, what's going on? Maybe I should leave."

He tore his gaze off Polly and said, "No way back now. Why are you uptight?"

I did have to stick it out. I felt smaller and smaller as it became more and more obvious to everyone that Matthew and Polly were an item, and I was a lump of clay.

We had to spend the night on the boat that night, too, and I was determined not to let anyone see that I was upset. It was one of the most humiliating situations I've ever been in. Matthew and Polly were kissing openly now.

That night, after a seasick Stacey crashed, Paul and Jane paired off on deck for some love talk, and Matthew and Polly wedged themselves in the bunk, giggling, yelling, "Stop it! You're tickling me!" until I thought I would throw myself overboard. Paul gave me a sympathetic look that made me feel doubly mortified.

In the morning, with Newport on the horizon, I was the first one off the boat and made a beeline for my car.

The car was unlocked, but I couldn't find my keys. I dumped my overnight bag out on the passenger seat, scrambling for my keys, when I heard a knock on the window.

It was Matthew. I didn't roll down my window, just kept looking for my keys.

I heard him yell, "Hey, Mary! Can I have a ride home? Everyone else has left, and there aren't any taxis!"

I found my keys. I took a deep breath, rolled down my window, and said, "You've got to be kidding."

Matthew, puzzled, said, "I think I put my house keys in your overnight bag, too. Did you find them?"

I pushed around the items on the passenger seat, found his keys, and said, "Yes. I did. Here." I threw them at him and drove off. It wasn't much, but it was better than nothing.

And it was that small act of revenge I turned to six months later when I found out that Matthew and Polly were getting married on his sailboat, joined by Paul and Jane for a slow cruise to Cape Cod where, the story goes, they say their love was forged.

—Mary, 28, caterer, Newport, Rhode Island

✳ ✳ ✳

Singing waiters and waitresses made the restaurant more fun. They came by the tables, singing hits from *Phantom of the Opera* and *Les Misérables.* My date said she was having a great time.

Our Caesar salads arrived, and I took a closer look at mine. Those were three odd-looking anchovies. I leaned closer, and rasped, "Roaches."

My date yelled, "Oo!" and used her fork to push them around.

My stomach turned. There were three big, dead roaches decorating my Caesar salad.

My date and I sifted through her salad, finding it uninfested.

I signaled over a waiter who was in the middle of the second verse of *Oklahoma!* and said, "Sorry about interrupting you. You're great. But there are three roaches on top of my Caesar salad."

He said, "Wow. That's wild. I'll bring you a new one."

I said, "My date doesn't want hers, either. And we don't want more salads, thank you. We're nauseated."

He took our salads, and returned with a platter of oysters. "On the house," he said.

Normally, I loved oysters, but the sight of those slimy things coming on the heels of our roaches didn't sit well with us, so we pushed the platter away. What I wanted was to be able to skip paying, and get the heck out of there.

Our waiter was coming our way, balancing a huge platter over his head, bellowing *The Sound of Music,* with great fanfare. He was passing our table, and I flagged him. Still singing, he nodded. The tray slipped, and hundreds of strands of spaghetti—six platefuls—spilled all over my date and me.

We stood up, yelping. Following our roach scare, this felt like a truck had backed up and dumped worms, blood, and guts on us.

Our waiter, holding his empty tray, said, "Will there be anything else? . . . Just kidding. Sorry about that."

—Dwight, 34, pediatrician, West Virginia

✻ ✻ ✻

Prom dresses were not easy to find last year. The dress couldn't be flashy, but it couldn't be as boring as a bridesmaid dress. It had to be fancier than a basic fun dress, but comfortable enough to dance in.

After months of shopping. I settled on a beige, lacy, vintage dress. It stopped a few inches above my knee, was strapless, and had some unusual bustier kind of top built into the bodice that made my breasts look bigger, and seemed to squeeze them up around my neck. Aside from the fact that it was uncomfortable to move my arms, I liked it.

My date and I got into the limousine he'd rented for the night, and we were off to the prom.

The dress started to disintegrate after two hours. It was hot in the ballroom, and I was covered with perspiration from dancing seven songs nonstop. Along with the fact that the dress was old, the humid conditions probably encouraged it to begin falling apart. The good news was that as the lace fell away, the bustier thing held fast and was made of thick, tough fabric.

My date flipped a loose piece of lace over my shoulder and said, "You know, that dress is kind of sexy." When a row of lace at the hem fell off, shortening the dress, he gamely said, "That dress is like no other. It keeps evolving through the night."

I was a little upset—I was afraid the dress would completely fall apart—but if my date was going to be a good sport, so was I.

We got back into the limousine to go to an after-prom party. My date took a silver flask from the inside pocket of his tuxedo jacket and offered it to me.

"Want a sip?"

I didn't drink alcohol, which he knew, so I refused.

The limousine driver said, "Pal. Hey! There's no drinking in the limo unless you buy one of our party bottles. Open the bar back there."

We did. Inside were rows of tiny liquor bottles and packets of peanuts and candy.

The driver said, "Anything you take from there, you pay for."

My date said, "That's okay. I brought my own," and took a long drink from his flask.

The driver said, "Let's not argue. Those are the rules. No drinking liquor you bring into the limo. No exceptions."

My date said, "Really?" and took an exaggerated drink from his flask. He added, "I paid for a limousine, not a chaperone."

I was stunned and said, "Stop it. Just put your flask away till we get to the party."

My date told the driver, "You should have told me in advance. It's my prom night. I'll do what I want. You just concentrate on the driving."

I said, "There's no need for a fight. Just put your flask away for five more minutes."

The driver slammed on the brakes and started to come around the limo to the back passenger side.

My date said, "Uh-oh."

His door opened, and the driver said, "Get out, guy. She can stay."

My date said, "Hey, I'm the one who paid for this thing, not her. I'm staying. Get back in and drive."

They started shouting at each other. The driver's big hand grabbed my date by the shirt collar and hauled him out of the limo, then the driver got back in and sped away, jostling me around in the back seat.

The driver said, "So, why him?"

I said, "Why you? That was my prom date you just threw out of the car."

The driver shrugged, and raced me to the party. Over an hour later my date showed up, tired from walking two miles before he could flag a ride. That was my sweet memory of prom night, sitting around in a disintegrating dress, waiting to see if my prom date could find his way to the party.

—Natalie, 17, student, Kansas

✳ ✳ ✳

Sleep. That's all I wanted. I was at a big party with my date, Howard, and I'd had too much to drink. The room was tipping, and I couldn't find him. I wandered through the huge house looking for him, and found a bedroom. I planned to lie down for just a second, until things stopped spinning, but I must have dozed off.

When I woke up, there was a guy snoring beside me. I took a close look. It was the host, Brent. I wobbled to the door, and saw a little black-and-white TV screen built into the wall. On the screen, I could see the party in progress downstairs.

I held onto the doorjamb, and Howard appeared. He looked at me, looked at Brent, and said, "What's going on? You're having sex with the host at his party while I'm downstairs?"

Brent woke up, heard Howard yelling at me, and said, "It's not like that all. But get her out of here."

Howard stalked away, and I followed at a snail's pace.

I found Howard dancing with a girl in a tight dress, and I walked up to him and said, "Let's talk."

Howard jerked away from my hand and said, "Let me introduce you to my date, Monique."

His date?

"I'm your date," I said, "and I want to talk to you."

Howard ignored me, and I found my purse and jacket and

walked to the vestibule. It's not like me, but I burst into tears and cried, "Life is hopeless!"

I decided I had to fight to the end to get my date back.

I had only taken two steps when I saw Howard and Brent walking toward me from opposite ends of the room.

Once they got to me, Brent said, "Howard, does your date always fall asleep at parties?"

Howard said, "I don't know, Brent. Do you always sleep with your friends' dates? How about you, Edie? Are you always in such a hurry to dump your date because you can't wait to sleep with the host?"

Something in me snapped.

I said, "Where do either of you adolescents get off accusing me of anything? I was in bed first. Brent had to have seen me there, so why don't you ask him why he laid down beside me? Furthermore—"

Brent cut me off and said, "Because that's my bedroom. You were sleeping in my bed."

I said, "This isn't the story of the three little bears. You could have slept somewhere else. And Howard, you're a jerk to think anything happened. Where were you, anyway, for an hour? Who's Monique? What were you doing with her? You and Brent deserve each other for friends."

One of Brent's friends appeared and said, "Hey, do you know that we were all watching you two snore on the closed-circuit TV? It was boring. We're in the rec room, listening to your fight, but the sound isn't good. Could you all speak up, and, you know, get really mad."

I said, "Closed-circuit TV? Does this mean we're being taped, too?"

Brent shrugged.

Howard said, "Is there a closed-circuit camera in that little exercise room, too?"

Brent said, "Yeah."

Howard looked ill.

I said, "You've probably got film of him doing something

naughty with Monique. This gets worse and worse. I'm out of here."

The worst part, I thought, wasn't that I was watched having a fight, it was that somewhere, in some grotesque film collection of Brent's, there was footage of me snoring and drooling.

—Edie, 25, hotel clerk, Nevada

* * *

My mother made me do it. I said I'd escort her friend's daughter to a ball in Philadelphia, even though we all lived in New Jersey.

The party was in a hotel ballroom on a Friday night. Ivy and I would spend the night—in separate rooms—and then we'd go home the next day. Aside from the fact that she and I didn't hit it off on the phone, my biggest reservation was that I'd be traveling in the crush of Christmas—leaving December 23rd, returning December 24th. I wasn't looking forward to racing up and down the East Coast in less than twenty-four hours, but I would have felt too guilty to refuse.

After work on Friday, I met Ivy at the train station. I wanted to take the 9:00 P.M. express, but she insisted on the local, which was obviously slower, and I gave in, even though we'd have to switch trains somewhere in Pennsylvania.

We made awkward conversation all the way to our first connection, where we disembarked and waited on the platform. A loudspeaker announced that our connection was delayed. Since I'd been in the same suit for twelve hours, I told Ivy I was going to the restroom to change into my tuxedo. She told me I couldn't. Her reason: She couldn't change into her dress because it was velvet, and would crush if she sat in it. Who'd know? She'd change at the party and wanted me to wait, too.

We waited forty-five minutes for our connection. We arrived in Philadelphia at 11:30 P.M. and jumped into a taxi. It died the second we got on the expressway. We hauled out our suitcases and garment bags and began thumbing. After a half-hour, a taxi picked us up.

We got to the ballroom at midnight, but we were still stuck. Her cousins were supposed to have left our keys at the front desk, but they had kept them, and were somewhere in the ballroom. The usher at the door wouldn't let us enter the dance because we weren't dressed for it.

We changed clothes in the lobby restrooms, leaving our bags at the front desk. By then we were both so irritated that we could barely look at each other.

We found her cousins, who talked with clenched jaws and, after giving us our keys, promptly ditched us.

The music was horrible. The friends she wanted us to hang out with had left, so we sat at a table alone and watched the action while she got drunk on white wine and I majored in vodka.

Her cousins finally asked us to join them at their table, and my date caught up on family gossip with them for two hours while I drummed the table with my fingers.

Realizing I could be on my way home, I said good night, expecting a struggle, but she wished me a safe trip and waved goodbye. I paid for my room, left her return train ticket for her at the desk, collected my bags, and got a cab to the station.

I missed the last train to New Jersey by three minutes. The next one wasn't until 6:00 A.M.

I sat on a bench, still in my tuxedo, and decided to sleep until the train arrived.

At 4:00 A.M., a homeless woman was nudging me awake.

"Wake up!" she said, while I rubbed my eyes and tried to remember why I was in a strange train station in a tuxedo. "That man took your bags and your wallet!"

The station police retrieved my things, arrested the man, and made sure I got on the 6:00 A.M. train.

When I got to my parents' house, I hadn't set my bags down before my mother said, "Perfect timing! It's Ivy on the phone. She wants to wish you a happy holiday. Here! Take the phone and talk to her. Oh, you're in your tuxedo! You look great! Here! Here's Ivy!"

I took the phone, and while my mother watched my face and listened, I said, "Me too . . . it was great . . . no, getting back was no trouble, certainly no more trouble than getting there was . . ."

—Russell, 31, finance, New Jersey

* * *

One of my friends kept telling me about her boyfriend's pal Marshall, and how we should go out. Marshall was a piano player.

One summer, I finally agreed. From my friend's description, I had expected a malnourished artist who was a little spacy. Instead, the guy at my door was healthy, in great shape, and looked sporty. He was actually attractive.

Our plans were to go to the beach on Saturday for a barbecue, just the two of us, and it had sounded like a fun way to get to know each other. Even if we'd didn't click, we'd at least be able to enjoy the beach.

He and I had an iced tea, and I was pretty sure I liked him, as far as a blind date goes anyway. He was a little laidback, kind of cool, not trying overly hard, but still a little nervous. We were just about to get going when my phone rang.

It was my sister. Over the phone she told me that I had to pick up my niece from day care and drive her home. My sister said she and her husband were studying for tests, and that I had to do this for them. I refused, explaining that I was on my way out the door with my date, but my sister was relentless. I checked with Marshall, who said he didn't mind if it wouldn't take very long, and I scribbled down the day-care address.

We got in Marshall's car and picked up my niece Brittany. On the way to my sister's, the traffic was so bad that we were at a standstill most of the time, with Brittany whining that she had to go to the bathroom. Through it all, Marshall was mellow and affable, even though I was uptight that our errand was taking so long.

When we got to my sister's house, the front door was locked, so we went around back, and there, in full swing, was a pool party. The music was going, people were splashing, my brother-in-law was bouncing on the diving board, and my sister was pouring piña coladas.

My sister said that it was an impromptu party for a neighbor's engagement, so I couldn't get too furious. But I told her that she had put Marshall and I off course by about two hours.

I was still miffed when Marshall and I got back in the car, He said that we still had plenty of time, and even though he was acting as nice as he could, I could tell that he was a little annoyed. We had to go to his parents' house, where he lived, to pick up the barbecue fixings, then we'd be off to the beach.

At the house, I met Marshall's parents and his eight brothers, two sisters, sisters- and brothers-in-laws, nieces and nephews. Everyone was great about the fact that when they asked how Marshall and I met, I'd say, "We're on a blind date."

It was a lot of family, but it was Saturday, and seemed like a good day for everyone to drop by. On the dining room table was a huge spread of delicious food.

Marshall led me into the kitchen, and he took marinated fish out of the refrigerator along with lentil salad, rice salad, a green salad, a bottle of wine, and a box of chocolates. I loaded everything in the cooler while he went to the garage to get the portable grill and charcoal.

I was admiring the salads when Marshall's father proudly said, "Marshall made all that himself last night," and he beamed.

I was starving, and I could tell that the barbecue was going to be great.

I helped Marshall load the car with a beach umbrella, blankets, and other things. His mother was still talking to me when

Marshall yelled something to me. His mom and I laughed at his enthusiasm, and I said, "Okay!" and got in the car beside Marshall.

The beach was beautiful. It didn't matter that driving my niece around had turned this into a sunset barbecue rather than a late-afternoon barbecue. The sky and water were magnificent blues. We sat on the blankets and watched the sun go down, drinking soda and swapping spring break stories. The date was finally going smoothly, instead of frantically.

Marshall said he was going to unload the car. He came back with the grill, charcoal, and wine, but no food.

Worried, he said, "I looked all over the car. Where'd you put the cooler with the food in it?"

I said, "Huh? Me? What about the cooler?"

Marshall said, "Right before we left, I asked you to grab the cooler off the kitchen counter and bring it."

I mumbled, "Oh no. I didn't hear you . . ."

We sat on the blanket, both feeling terrible.

I said, "We could go back to your house for the food."

But he said that wasn't a good idea, because by the time we got back, the beach would be closed.

I apologized, and he apologized, and we sat on the blanket. I felt like an idiot and wanted to bury my head in the sand.

We decided to go back to his house anyway, and find something to eat. The half-hour drive seemed to take hours.

Marshall and I walked in the back door, and there, on the kitchen table, was a huge birthday cake. His family was gathered around it, and a guy who looked just like Marshall was smiling at us from the other side of the table.

"I'm Marshall's twin, Matthew," he introduced himself.

I looked at the cake. It read, HAPPY BIRTHDAY, MATTHEW AND MARSHALL.

I said, "Marshall, it's your birthday, too?"

And he nodded.

His father said, "So, Marshall, you decided you'd spend your birthday with the family after all?"

Oh, boy. Marshall had blown off a family get-together to go on a date with me, and so far I'd managed to sabotage all his plans. This was some birthday Marshall was having.

His mother lit the candles, and both guys blew them out amid great applause.

Marshall said, "Mom, we're starving," and his mother pulled us into the kitchen, where she unwrapped all the food she'd put away, reheating generous portions for us.

I realized that the family was waiting for us to finish eating so that the twins could open presents.

I ate my slice of birthday cake while the guys opened mountains of gifts.

Thirty minutes later, Marshall's mother said, "I can't bear to watch this. Marshall, I know you'd rather be out on your date. Go!" His father agreed, and the whole family waved goodbye as if we were newlyweds.

We had coffee at a little outdoor café, not saying much, then Marshall took me home.

Marshall gave me a kiss on the cheek, and I apologized again and wished him happy birthday.

He smiled and said, "Thanks. It wasn't so bad, really. Well ... I'll call you."

I never heard from him again. Can you blame him? Date me, date *my* family.

—Lizzie, 28, waitress, Virginia

✳ ✳ ✳

This Halloween, I was LaToya Jackson, with giant hair, a short tight top, tight pants, and stiletto heels, with a Michael Jackson mask. My conversation was, "As his sister, all I can say is, maybe Michael did it."

My date called and said he was running late, and would I take the subway up to East 89th, where he lived. I lived on 3rd Street, and we were supposed to go to two parties, including one a few blocks from me. I figured we would go to the party near him first.

So at ten at night I got on the subway with the other people in costume and rode to his apartment.

He wasn't home. Walking like LaToya, on those shoes, wasn't easy, and I'd had to walk four blocks from the subway station, so I sat on his stoop and waited.

At a pay phone, I checked my answering machine, finding a message from him. He had to help a friend finish his costume, and wanted me to meet him at an apartment on West 72nd. I wanted to scream. He sounded sincere, so I walked to the bus stop, taking it across town, then transferring to a downtown bus.

I rang the buzzer, but no one answered. A note was taped to the door. It was for me. I opened it and read, "We waited. Where are you? We're worried. Call us, or come over."

The address was five blocks away, so I walked there, cursing him under my breath. If I hadn't gone to all the trouble to pull together a costume, I would have gone home two apartments ago.

At the address, the doorman told me there wasn't anyone living there by the name I gave, and he wouldn't let me in.

By then I was so tired that I hailed a taxi and went home. There was a message on my answering machine from my date.

"We're back at my apartment. We thought it would be easier for you to just come here. Come over! We're waiting for you!"

I didn't know if it was supposed to be a trick or a treat, but I took off my costume, watched TV, and listened to my machine pick up his next three messages, each one directing me to a new address.

Trick.

—Vivian, 30, air traffic controller, New York City

* * *

Jacques and I were inseparable. He loved that I was from Arkansas, I loved that he was from Belgium. At first, because of our dueling accents, we didn't understand a thing the other said. He was thirty-three, in the diamond business, and never married—"Though I vant to be," he murmured in my ear, adding that he'd always dreamed of having children, and wanted to have lots of little girls who looked like me.

I was beyond ecstatic after our fifth date. He'd practically proposed! I couldn't wait for him to meet my sister.

My sister shook hands with him when we all met for dinner, then whispered in my ear, "He's got the look of a divorced guy."

I whispered back, "What are talking about? You're crazy."

When Jacques took a break from charming my sister and went to the men's room, my sister said, "He's got that white-collar criminal element. You know, barely shifty, but shifty. He dresses too well. Only a guy who had a wife who did his shopping would have this much taste. He's too used to it."

I held up my hand to stop her, and she said, "He's too comfortable around women. He's not a bit nervous."

I wanted to kill her. She always found something wrong with my boyfriends.

I said, "You're on."

Two months after we'd been dating, my car conked out. Jacques came to my rescue.

"Zon't worry," he said, "I know of a geem of a cah just for you."

He was right. It was a two-year-old green sports car with a tan leather interior that was in perfect shape and drove like a dream. It belonged to a friend of his who was moving back to Belgium and needed to sell it fast. I closed the deal for only six thousand dollars cash.

A month later, I went to Belgium with Jacques to meet his family. If this wasn't heading toward marriage, what was?

First stop was his aunt's house for lunch. The aunt's daughter and her little son dropped by.

After lunch, his aunt said, "I'm so glad that Jacques is getting married again."

I said, "Again?"

His aunt said, "Did I say again? No, I didn't. I said, a sin.
It's a sin that he's never married. More wine?"

Jacques's little nephew climbed onto his lap, tugging at
Jacques's ears, squirming, and screaming, and Jacques stayed
relaxed. He was comfortable holding the child and didn't freak
at the child's tantrum. I thought, *He's a natural father.*

Late that afternoon we were shopping for jewelry, with
Jacques asking my opinion of diamond solitaires, which made
me feel bubbly. As we were leaving the shop, a man called
Jacques's name. They traded greetings on the crowded sidewalk, and I didn't feel like stepping into their meeting.

The friend said, "You missed all the university reunions.
Come to the next one! It's in three years. We'll all be fifty and
ancient! How's your little girl? She should be a teenager now,
no? Got to go!"

I stood on the sidewalk and thought. That was too much information to take in. What was the first thing the friend had
said? Jacques steered me into a crowded café and ordered
lunch, chattering about diamonds.

I said, "You're forty-seven? You have a teenage daughter?
You were married? Is this true? Why didn't you tell me?"

"Vell," said Jacques, sipping his wine matter-of-factly, "eet
depends. Eet was a very long time ago."

He convinced me that he had been embarrassed to tell me
because he came from a conservative family that never got
over having a divorce in the family. He talked and talked until
I realized that although I was upset, I was going to forgive
him. Especially when he slipped the engagement ring on my
finger.

Back home, a week later, I was on the way to meet Jacques
for lunch to talk about what kind of wedding we wanted.

On impulse, I swung into a car dealership. I'd been thinking of selling the sports car. I had already gotten two speeding

tickets, and I also wanted a less expensive car to maintain. The profit I'd get would make Jacques and me very happy. I drove it in for an estimate.

"How much will you give me?" I asked, knowing I'd sell the car for a bundle.

The mechanic's once-over lasted a half-hour. Then he conferred with the dealer, and they walked slowly toward me.

"It's a great car, isn't it?" I asked. They weren't going to trick me.

The mechanic pawed the ground with his shoe, and the dealer said, "Ma'am, are you aware that this car has spent time underwater?"

I pointed to my chest and said, "*My* car? How can a car spend time underwater?"

The dealer spelled it out: "It was totaled. Then rebuilt and the chassis repaired. See here? And here? And back here?"

The mechanic pointed and said, "And over here."

I followed them around the car, gasping.

The mechanic pointed under the car and said, "See all that rust? Must have had a wreck and then fallen in a lake and stayed on the bottom for some time. It's highly interesting."

The dealer put his hand out and said, "I'm sorry, but we're not interested. Your best bet is to hang on to it until it gives out, which it probably will in a few years. They put a junky engine in it. How's it run on the highway?"

"Just great," I mumbled, shaking his hand and getting in the car.

The fact that my dream car had spent some time underwater pushed me over the brink.

Jacques had lied from start to finish. I was stuck with the car, so I kept the ring and I told Jacques to take a hike. Looking back, the worst part wasn't that he had a teenage daughter and an ex-wife. It was the fact that my car had spent some time underwater. That was definitely highly interesting—and humiliating.

There's one thing I haven't done yet, and that's to have the ring appraised.

—Elizabeth, 25, accountant, San Antonio

* * *

Lucy's fight for righteousness knew no boundaries. She could take a stand on anything she believed in, and you'd better look out.

We went to the movies, and we hadn't gotten past the opening credits when the screen went black. The lights went on, and an usher announced that the projector had broken and there wouldn't be a movie.

Everybody groaned. The usher said we'd each get a complimentary ticket if we'd form a line.

There was lots of grumbling. The line was barely moving. Lucy said, "I'm going up front to see what's going on."

When she made this kind of announcement, it was usually the kiss of death, so I said, "Stay here," and she ignored me and took off.

After five minutes, the line came to a complete halt, and the word buzzed down the line that there was a crazy woman up front causing a scene. I had a horrible idea who it was, and walked to the front of the line.

There was Lucy, confronting the manager and assistant manager, yelling, "We all deserve a cash refund *and* free tickets, and I won't let the line move until you give it to us. We're entitled to it! Comp tickets aren't good enough."

The people at the front of the line were noncommittal, simply listening. At the very least, they'd get a ticket. If Lucy won, they'd also get cash. No reason for them not to wait, but no reason to get involved, either.

Management kept refusing, and Lucy started screaming, "You're cheating us! You're cheating us! I won't let the line move until you cough up!"

The manager said that if she didn't accept her comp ticket and let the line move, he'd call the police.

She yelled, "Go ahead! It's the principle of the thing that you're missing! *You* screwed up and inconvenienced *us*!"

I said to the manager, "Just give us our money and we'll leave. Keep the tickets. That's a good compromise, isn't it?"

Lucy was furious, but the manager agreed. Their cash box was closed, and the manager looked in his wallet, saying all he had on him were two five-dollar bills and five singles. He handed me the money, and I dragged Lucy to the corner.

She said, "You ruined everything! I was making headway! Why did you interfere? I hate you!"

I was barely listening, counting my money.

I said, "Hey, he was supposed to give me five singles, but I think he only gave me two."

Lucy stopped yelling at me to say, "He shortchanged you? That's it. That's the last straw. We have to go back and straighten this out. Come on."

I said, "Forget about it. I'm sorry I mentioned it. We're not going back."

Lucy said, "You're right. I'm going to use this pay phone to call the police about the theater."

I pleaded with her not to, and when she picked up the receiver, I said, "If you make that call, I'm leaving. I mean it."

She glared at me, started dialing, and I left, heading to her apartment.

An hour went by, and the phone rang. It was Lucy's mother. She said, "You'd better clear out of there. Lucy's dad and I are with her at the theater, and there's a big scene. The manager tried to have the police arrest Lucy, and only her dad could persuade them not to. And she's crying her eyes out that you deserted her, and her dad wants to kill you. If I were you, I'd get out of the apartment right now. We're on our way over."

I didn't need convincing. I shut off the TV, hung up the

phone, and grabbed my jacket in one fluid motion and ran out the door. I doubled locked my door at home.

The next day, Lucy called, sounding terse and ready to explode. She said, "You'd better hurry if you want your stuff. I threw it all out the window and it's in the street getting picked over."

Frankly, no one seemed to want my albums, socks, or sweatshirts. As I was picking up the last of my things, a heavy sock came flying from her window and landed at my feet.

Inside was a note and a rock. The note, not surprisingly, said, "We're through."

Good. That meant I could catch that movie.

—Colin, 24, deejay, Arizona

* * *

7

✹ ✹ ✹ ✹

"D" Is for Danger

You're not just having a bad time, you're in trouble. When did your date begin acting so threatening? When did the situation "morph" into a horror movie? Safe in your room later, you have to admit that was a close call—but with the skill of a Houdini, you managed to wiggle out of it.

Catalina Island was a paradise. All that was missing was a date, and my friend Carol said it was arranged. While I'd been shopping alone, Carol, her husband, and another couple we traveled with had met a nice guy named Eric. They'd been waiting for a table, started talking to him, and asked him to join them. They reported that Eric had worked on Wall Street in the eighties and at forty had retired to California. He was divorced, had no kids, was handsome, nice, and amusing, and would join us for dinner that night.

I dreaded a fix-up, but I was in the mood for a date, so I agreed.

Eric was exactly as promised. Though from New York, he was the perfect California man: blond, longish hair, in great shape, and looked about thirty. He and I went out for drinks after dinner, and he took me for a drive in his new Porsche convertible.

He liked that I was an entertainment lawyer, having dabbled in entertainment investments himself, and invited me to his house the next weekend, promising there would be other house guests.

On the agreed-upon weekend, he called, saying I should meet him at a restaurant and follow him to his house, since there were a lot of turns and unmarked roads.

I followed him for about a half-hour before we stopped in front of giant Gothic gates that blocked a road. Huge letters that crested the gates bore his initials. We were clearly at an estate, not a house.

He got out of his car, came around to mine, and said, "You might want to leave your car here and drive up with me. The rains washed out a lot of my drive, and it's full of craters."

Since I had a new Lexus that I pampered, I agreed, tossing my gear in his tiny back seat.

He was right; the dirt road was torn up, and I was glad it was his car and not mine that was taking a beating.

The car climbed a tall hill, and at the top was a rusty, small green trailer. Dogs barked like they were waking the dead.

We got out of the car, and I skimmed the horizon, searching for the mansion.

"Here it is!" exclaimed Eric, throwing his arms wide. "Come see this."

I slung my bags over my shoulders and followed. We were at the base of a huge slab of foundation.

"This is where my house is going to be!" he said. "Ten thousand square feet."

I nodded, and said, "That's a lot of concrete. I've never seen a foundation that big before. Impressive. . . . Uh, where's the house your friends and I'll be sleeping in?"

I never expected the reply.

"In the trailer," he said, "soon as I let out the dogs."

He opened the trailer door, and three Doberman pinschers bounded for me, howling and growling.

"Missy! June Bug! Harold! Down! Down! Get down! Oh well. Don't worry. They don't bite. Just stay near the trailer and don't excite them. I want to check any mischief they might have done inside while I was gone. Be right back."

I planted myself on the ground, looking over the top of the trailer so I wouldn't make the wrong kind of eye contact with the dogs. They were circling and nosing me.

Eric opened the trailer door and said, "Wait for me! Don't walk over here alone; the dogs look a little spooked."

Inside, the trailer was a bigger dump than outside. It was tidy, but about thirty years old. He lit a kerosene lamp, since there was no electricity, and I said, "Where are the other guests?"

I wasn't too surprised when he said they weren't coming. If I had known the arrangements, I wouldn't have come either.

I said, "I think I'll be heading back soon."

He said, "Okay. Would you join me in a drink first?"

Over our drinks, as we clinked glasses, he said, "I've been on a spaceship. I've been operated on by aliens. In fact, they implanted a device on me, a tracking instrument so they know where to locate me for the next time they beam me up."

I drank my drink in one swallow, and held it out for a refill. I believe there are higher life forms in the universe, and I suppose that from time to time they do a little nosing around, checking us out. I read the book and saw the movie *Communion,* so I could imagine how creepy it must have been.

He said, "I have a video of the experience that they gave me. Would you like to see it?"

I nodded. I knew someone who might be interested in his story. The female lead could be Julia Roberts, and the male lead could be Kevin Costner, Tom Cruise, or—

Coming to my senses, I said, "First, tell me—how long a walk is it to my car? Two miles, three?"

"Three," he said.

I grabbed my bags and said, "I think I'll take a little walk."

Eric said, "Okay. But stay close to the trailer. That way the dogs won't bother you. And this property used to be an ancient burial site. Every time the dogs dig, they turn up a bone or two, and there's this story about a witch who roams when bones are disturbed. I haven't seen her in a couple of days. But I saw the other ones last night. Every time the dogs dig, they release evil spirits."

I stayed calm. So far, he wasn't dangerous, just delusional. I said, "I'm gonna go home now."

I expected protests.

He said, "Okay. I'll drive you."

"No," I said, stepping outside. "I'll walk." I didn't really want to walk alone after hearing that silly but scary story, but I didn't want to be in his control in the car either.

"I insist," he said. "You'll be safer with me. Tomorrow we can meet for lunch."

"Right!" I said, staring into the darkness, realizing that the night was so thick now that I couldn't see the road.

The ride down the road was slow, but uneventful. We talked about movies, and I was starting to wonder if my mind had been playing tricks on me, if he was mostly normal after all.

When we got to the gate, his headlights cut through the fog and caused my car to look like it was floating, which made me gasp.

I screamed when I looked at Eric. He had pulled a huge knife from under his seat, was staring at me with glazed eyes, and said, "Don't worry. I won't hurt you. This is for the werewolf that lives around here. He's probably waiting for you."

I wanted to disappear or start running and screaming.

I knew I shouldn't panic, that I wasn't with a sinister man but an odd man. *Accept him on his own terms,* I decided.

"Thank you for the protection," I said. "I'll follow you."

Out of the car, I heard a howl and braced for the werewolf. I realized it was the echo of his dogs at the trailer. Eric cocked his head and said, "You better hurry. He's coming," and held open my door.

First I checked my trunk and back seat, then scrambled into my car, my adrenaline pumping, my legs shaky. I had started to believe this guy's fantasies.

"Should I wait for you to close the gate and get back in your car?" I asked, starting my car, trying to avoid watching him get attacked by the werewolf.

Eric shook his head, looking over the top of the car, not at me, and said, "I can take care of myself. It's you I'm worried about. Go. Get out of here. Go!"

I burned rubber reversing, and tore out of there clutching the wheel. I fumbled for the car phone, knocking it to the floor in my panic before I could hold it steady. Who would I dial? Who could I tell this story to who would believe me? Better yet, why was I believing the story? Even better yet, why in the world had I ever let myself be fixed up again? It always turned out like this. I slowed down, turned on the radio, peered through the windshield at the full moon, and said, "Never again. Never again."

—Christine, 42, entertainment lawyer, Los Angeles

＊ ＊ ＊

Jackpot! It was the early eighties in Manhattan, and I'd just inherited a fortune from an obscure relative who lived in Europe whom I'd never even met, and I had money coming out of all my pockets. I didn't have any idea what to do with it all, but I knew how to start.

I called Debbie, who was also a lawyer, and asked her out. We'd already had one date, and it had been decent but boring. Since I wanted to paint the town and I needed a date, I thought it was too soon to give up on her.

First stop was a downtown club that used to be a bath-house. Geraldo Rivera was there filming the club, and patrons started misbehaving for the cameras.

Debbie and I had finished our third drink and were wandering around downstairs where there was a big sunken stone bath. A guy materialized out of nowhere, clutched Debbie by the waist, and pulled her into the bath with him. The action in the bath was raucous, and I roamed around the rim, hunting for Debbie. Guys were grabbing at her, and she was flailing around, splashing at them. When she waved at me, I knew she was all right. She stood up, and my mouth flopped open. So did hers. She wasn't wearing her blouse or her bra. She sank back into the water, but no one seemed to notice. In fact, that's when we noticed that a couple of men and women were nude.

I took off my jacket and held it for her to slip into. She wrung out her long blond hair out and said, "That was a blast!"

I said, "What about your shirt? Shouldn't we try to find it?"

Someone threw her shoes to us and she put them on.

Debbie said, "Let's have fun! To heck with my blouse and anything else that happens! Let's get a drink!"

She was loosening up. She was standing there in my jacket, with its one button closing in the vicinity of her navel, the hem a few inches from her knees. You couldn't see her skirt. Her eyes were shining.

After our fifth drink, I said, "Now let's do the uptown thing!" and she said, "I'm game!"

At ten-thirty, we went to a pricey restaurant that was a docked boat. I had been afraid that we couldn't get in considering the way Debbie was dressed, but in fact her outfit got us the best table upstairs, under the stars.

We ordered anything we wanted, and I also ordered a bottle of champagne.

"Bring us the best!" I told the happy waiter, and told Debbie, "I've always wanted to say that!"

We were having my kind of a dream night—I liked one streak of wildness in any big night out.

After our astronomically priced dinner, we walked to the nearby helicopter pad. It was midnight, and I felt like a ride in the sky.

I said, "Take us for the best ride in Manhattan that money can buy!"

We'd only been in the air two minutes before Debbie said, "Oh, no. I feel sick."

The pilot handed her a doggie bag.

I yelled to the pilot, "I don't want to land yet! What should we do?"

The pilot gave Debbie some Pepto-Bismol tablets, and her stomach settled. The ride was beautiful, and we had a smooth landing.

We were feeling subdued—because of the magic of the ride, and mostly because Debbie was still peaked. We walked a few blocks and she said, "The night air really helps. I feel a lot better. I want more action."

I said, "Me, too," and we hailed a cab. I directed the driver downtown.

Wanting the most crazed night possible, we went to a sleazy bar off the beaten track in the East Village. We danced to the jukebox and drank until we could barely stand.

When we left, at three in the morning, we saw four skinheads sitting on the curb, shooting us dirty stares.

Feeling my oats, I said, "Look at those guys."

Debbie said, "They're just punks with guitars. Punks."

I said, "Punks. Bunch of punks. *Punks!*"

One of them kicked me in the face, knocking out my two new porcelain veneers and giving me a mild concussion. I had a moment of clarity when I realized Debbie and I were in serious trouble. Another of them—a skinhead girl—belted Debbie in the face, busting her lip, before shoving her to the ground.

In the ambulance, Debbie and I were holding hands. My

clothes were caked in blood. When we were taken into the emergency room, we requested side-by-side gurneys and held hands there, too, while they stitched us up. Debbie recovered easily, but I saw double for two weeks.

The policeman who took our report said, "You're lucky that's all that happened to you. You could have gotten hurt a lot worse, maybe even killed, you two, know that? You were asking for trouble."

Debbie and I looked at each other and nodded, realizing that we had capped our big night out with danger, split lips, concussions, a police report, and the ominous opinion that we were lucky to be alive. That was some night.

We dated for almost two years, but then we drifted apart. I guess the relationship just wasn't exciting anymore.

—Brandon, 27, lawyer, Manhattan

✳ ✳ ✳

Spin the bottle was old hat for us. We'd been a foursome since nursery school—Ned, Jamie, Alexie, and me. Now the girls—Jamie and Alexie—were almost twelve. Ned and I had just turned eleven. The girls were a little advanced on us and had abandoned spin the bottle last year, even though Ned and I thought it was still terrific. Mostly Ned and I liked going into a dark closet and making monster noises, which never got a scare out of Jamie or Alexie, no matter how much we tried. These days the girls thought our ideas were silly.

Jamie came up with the idea of going on a double date. It didn't matter who was on a date with whom; if the four of us went together and called it a double date, she said, then it was. It was time to be grown-up about love. She decided we would all go into Manhattan and visit the F.A.O. Schwartz toy store— the store of our dreams.

Ned and I thought it was a fantastic idea. It would be exciting, since we'd be going into Manhattan from New Jersey. I remember Alexie saying, "We shouldn't do it. We're going to get in trouble in the city. It's dangerous. Let's stay home."

Jamie's mother dropped us off at the store, and said she'd meet us at the entrance in one hour. She was going across the street to shop, and that's all the time alone she'd give us.

The instant Jamie's mom left, we were excited to be on our own in a giant store crammed with goodies. We ran around, playing with everything.

Ned played with a small, portable pinball machine, and started showing off, throwing his shoulder around energetically every time he pressed the buttons that flung the flippers into play. He was also moving a big rubber ball back and forth across the floor with his right foot.

"Look at this, Jamie," he cried, courting his love. "Look at me! This isn't easy."

Jamie grimaced at him and clutched a teddy bear that was wearing a tuxedo to her chest.

I said, "Big deal," which made Ned nudge the ball further away from him.

I saw it in slow motion. While Ned was throwing himself into his pinball maneuvers, he accidentally kicked the ball into the legs of the pinball machine.

The pinball machine crashed to the floor one corner at a time, taking down a nearby display of trolls with it. The trolls tumbled into a rack of baby dolls, and they spilled onto Ned's head while he sat on the floor in a daze.

There was a moment of silence while we stared at him, then I heard Alexie scream, "Run, Victor! Run, Ned! Run, run!"

Out of the corner of my eye, I saw Ned scramble to his feet, but I was already off, running up the stairs, passing a collection of trains that looked like fun, and whizzing by trucks I would have liked to stop and touch.

I had to run! Ned and I were in trouble. We'd destroyed displays, and maybe broken the pinball machine. If a manager caught us, we could be arrested and thrown in jail. It would be hours before Jamie's mother figured out where we were and came to get us. The police might not even let us go for years. We were in big, big trouble.

My heart was pounding. I had to outwit them all! I had to hurry and find a way out of the store.

I raced by toy guns, but they were so cool that I slid to a stop and backed up to hold one in my hands and aim it.

When I put the gun back on its shelf, I had the first epiphany of my life. I thought, Why am I running? I didn't do anything wrong. Ned was the one who was in trouble. I could stop and play as long as I wanted.

Then I saw Ned, frantic, coming up behind me, yelling, "Run!" and I took off again. The fact that I had started running from the beginning made me look guilty. There was no way I could explain why I was running if I were innocent. I was as much a criminal as Ned now.

There was the front door. I was almost free! All I had to do was get through the stuffed animal department.

My feet kept going, but my body lifted off the floor, and I choked.

A big hand had grabbed my shirt collar from behind and lifted me up, then dropped me.

It was the authorities. I was sitting crumpled on the floor, trapped. His outfit was daunting: white shirt, black tie, black pants, big heavy black shoes, and name tag. I was a goner.

The authority said, "Hold it right there, kid. Where do you think you're going? What happened here?"

I gulped and looked around. I heard a big crash, and hoped that Ned wasn't heading my way. It would only make things worse.

I thought fast and said, "Nothing."

The man said, "What?"

I was shaking. I didn't want to rat out Ned, but I didn't want to go to prison either.

Jamie and Alexie were huddled not far away, eyes wide as

saucers, their mouths hanging open. I wanted to call to them, but didn't want to incriminate them.

The man said, "You destroyed an entire area of the store. What do you have to say for yourself?"

I stared hard at him, and said, "Nothing," hoping that would bail me out, realizing that it never did at home, so why would it would help here? My heart sank.

The man stood me up and said, "You're coming with me."

My chest wanted to explode in misery as he led me past the girls. Alexie had been right; this was a dangerous place for a date.

I stared at the floor, counting the blocks on the pattern to keep myself from going berserk.

The man opened the door, directed me onto the sidewalk, turned me to face him, and said, "Do not *ever* come back in here again, do you understand? I never forget a face, and next time I see you, you'll be in even bigger trouble."

I nodded, looking around on the sidewalk, praying that Mom and Dad would materialize and take me home.

Alexie and Jamie came out onto the sidewalk and stared at me. A few minutes later, Ned came racing, saying, "I made it! They didn't catch me! That was close! Did you see how I escaped?"

I said, "Good for you. I can't come back here again. They caught me."

Alexie said, "That's not true. The man said you can't come back without a parent."

Really? I shook my head. "That's not what I heard him say. I'm banned from the best toy store in the world."

Ned and Jamie exchanged glances, and Jamie said, "Don't be a baby."

Ned said, "Yeah, don't be a baby. We have a half-hour left. I'm going back in." To the girls, he said, "You want to come?" and to me he said, "Just wait here. We'll be back in ten minutes."

Ned and Jamie dashed back in. Alexie looked at me with pity, but she went in, too.

I stood outside, my nose pressed against the glass window, watching my double date vaporize. I was out there alone, and Ned was inside with his date and my date, and that's not far from how it went when we were in college either.

—Victor, 35, professor of physics, New Jersey

＊ ＊ ＊

A ctive blind dates were the best kind, I thought. That way, if the date didn't work out, at least there wouldn't be any downtime, and there'd be an activity to distract us.

Since it was early summer, I proposed a Saturday afternoon rowboating date at the pond near my house.

All I knew about my date, Susan, was that she worked in the beauty industry and was supposed to be outgoing.

It was a gorgeous summer day and I was early, so I went ahead and rented a boat. It was the kind of day you can't help but be happy on, even if your girlfriend called off the engagement two months ago. The sun was on my face, there was a little breeze, and the pond was pretty.

Someone was waving to me—I'd told her I'd be wearing a red windbreaker. I rowed toward shore.

Even though the weather was mild, Susan was wearing a beret, a winter coat, and big hiking boots.

I met her at the entrance to the rental area.

"Fred!" she called, coming toward me, straightening her horn-rimmed, thick black glasses that I'd seen on other people who wanted to let you know that they thought they were intellectuals.

I said, "Susan?"

She said, "Is this your boat?" and hopped in.

I got in, too, and rowed us to the middle of the pond.

"Aren't you hot?" I asked, curious about the snowstorm

outfit. I eyed her boots, wondering why anyone would go row-boating wearing what amounted to concrete boots. I hoped we wouldn't sink.

"Yes!" she said, peeling off her layers and tossing them onto the floor of the rowboat. She was wearing a tight Spandex jumpsuit underneath. She took off her beret, and springs of red hair popped straight up on top of her head.

She started telling me about a new breakthrough cream that was supposed to take inches of fat off thighs, and that she wouldn't write a big story on it until it was proven to be legit-imate, and I noticed that she was leaning toward me. I leaned away.

She went into a squat position, never taking her eyes off me, and leaned so far forward that I was leaning flat back. She tried to kiss me, and I ducked.

She came toward me again, and I ducked again. I didn't like her.

I said, "Be careful! You're tipping the boat!"

She kissed me on the lips, and I leaned aside, but she kissed me again.

I felt violated, and mad.

I said, "This is no place to be kissing," and she said, "There's no time like the present," and pressed me back for another kiss. Then she unzipped my windbreaker and tried to get it off me, but I kept firm hold on my oars to stop her.

"Cut it out," I said, flailing my oars. "Sit back. Stop it."

I pushed her away, and frantically started rowing for home.

She said, "Relax. You're overreacting. It's just a couple of kisses. Didn't you like it?"

Her glasses were tilted, and she looked like a demented sex demon in her outfit.

I didn't answer, just kept rowing.

She stood up, and lunged for me, and I don't know how I kept the boat from capsizing. She put her hands over my wrists to stop me from rowing, and I pushed her hands away. She was an octopus.

When we got to shore, I jumped out. I was huffing and puffing from rowing like there was no tomorrow.

She gave me a tough once-over, sort of sneered, and said, "What'd you invite me here for, if you didn't have the same thing in mind? You were asking for it."

Then she pulled her beret over her red sprockets, threw her sweaters and jacket over her arm, and walked off, shaking her head.

That was what I got for suggesting something as provocative as rowboating on a pond.

—Fred, 30, policeman, Boston

* * *

I had been grounded for a month, and the minute my penance was up, I accepted a date to go out with Griffin.

It was Saturday night, and Griffin had worked since nine in the morning at a restaurant, filling in for a friend by working two shifts. He was exhausted, but said that we would still go to a party.

We danced for hours, and at a quarter to twelve it was time for us to call it a night so I would make my midnight curfew.

As Griffin slowly drove me home, I chatted to him about what a great time I'd had, and I noticed that the car was veering left, eventually going over the yellow line. There weren't any cars on that side, but I yelled, "Griffin! Look out!"

When he didn't answer, I hit him on the shoulder with my right hand, and I steered the wheel with my left hand, shouting at him.

He'd fallen asleep! Finally he woke up, and I yelled, "Work the pedals! You work the pedals, and I'll drive!"

Together, we slowly drove like this for a mile before I was sure that Griffin was concentrating well enough to drive solo.

When we got to my parents' house, we both breathed a sigh of relief. I told Griffin not to turn off the engine, that he should go straight home. I asked if he wanted to come inside and sleep on the sofa, and he declined. I thanked him and got out of the car.

As I was walking up the sidewalk, I turned to wave goodbye, and couldn't believe my eyes.

Griffin's head was lying on the steering wheel, and the car was rolling forward, gaining speed on the slope, toward a fence.

I yelled, "Pull up your hand brake! Pull up your hand brake!"

Suddenly all the lights came on in my front yard.

I ran to Griffin's car and tried to open the passenger door.

I screamed at him to wake up and he did, yanking up the hand brake. The car stopped inches in front of the fence.

That was the good news.

The bad news was that my parents were furious that I came home past midnight, and for accepting a ride with someone who was too sleepy to drive. They made Griffin call home and sleep on our couch. And they grounded me for another month.

—Laura, 16, student, Michigan

✳ ✳ ✳

Some honor. I was on my way to Mexico with a group of fraternity brothers and their dates. I was one of the dates.

My sorority was proud of me. I was going out with the best guy in the best fraternity on the best date of the year—the fraternity's bus trip from New Mexico to Mexico.

Two hours into the trip, on a hot, stinky bus, my calm, churchgoing, teetotaling dean's list of a date had turned into a Jamaican-rum–soaked pig who kept pawing at me.

I looked around for the chaperones, and saw that they were

smashed, too. In fact, everyone on the bus—except for me— was drinking like a fish.

It was a horror. The plan was to spend two nights in Mexico before getting back on the bus to go home. I wondered if I'd really have my own room, like my date had promised. The situation had degenerated.

My date reached for the buttons on my blouse, and I hit his hands away. He pushed me back against the seat and started kissing my neck. I pushed him back so hard that he fell into the aisle.

"You're mine," he said, looking possessed.

I had been scared until that comment, then I got angry.

"I'm yours because I'm on a bus with your buddies and you're all drunk? I don't think so."

I stood on the seat, grabbed the overhead luggage rack, and pulled myself up, kicking aside overnight bags. I lay facedown, glaring at my date through the metal slats.

He stood up, said, "Come back here," and reached for my ankle.

I saw a wooden umbrella in front of me, grabbed it, and poked my date on the top of his head. He yelped in pain.

He reached for my waist, and I jabbed his ear with the tip of the umbrella. He was stunned.

When he reached for my leg, I pushed a heavy bag over the side and onto his head. He wobbled a little, looking confused. The bus cheered.

I hated them all. I rode to Mexico like that, lying on the luggage rack, periodically tossing bags onto my date or jabbing him with my umbrella. The drunker he got, the easier it got to nail him.

After twenty minutes, he said, "Stop. You're hurting me. I give up," and sat on the seat, drinking straight from his bottle of rum before he passed out.

My plan was simple. The first time the bus stopped, I'd grab my little overnight bag, get off the bus, and arrange my own transportation home.

The first stop was sooner than I thought. As we pulled up to a Mexican gas station, I grabbed my bag, planning to race down the aisle and be the first off. My date was waking up, mumbling my name.

I couldn't resist. I swung my overnight bag at his head, then held my umbrella on him like a rifle and said, "One false move and I'll get you where it counts."

He held up his hands like he was under arrest and said, "I give up. Just don't hurt me."

I ran off the bus, relieved to be rid of the sleaze, feeling victorious.

He was a sham, with no scruples. No good would ever come of him.

Ten years later, having just moved to a new town, I turned on the local news. There, running for mayor, was a pious candidate yelling about equal rights for minorities, homosexuals, and women. Who do you think it was? Yes. It was my date to Mexico. What a hypocrite! I turned to my husband and said, "Don't unpack."

—Teresa, 32, professor of behavioral sciences, North Dakota

❋ ❋ ❋

Ordinarily, a prison record would have bothered me. That's not the first description that would have rolled off my tongue if I were ticking off what I was looking for in a dream man. But I had been divorced for six months and hadn't been out on one date yet. My best friend had a cousin who was friends with Howard, who had just gotten out of prison. My best friend had said, "Howard is supposed to be a really nice guy who got a bad break in life. He might be a good guy to go out with once or twice, so you can get the hang of dating again. You married your high school sweetheart—at least have dinner with a guy you weren't in homeroom with. Just to get started."

That made sense to me.

Howard was reasonably attractive, twenty-nine, and did seem really sweet. He was dressed in a suit and took me to a good restaurant, which was sweet. He opened my car door and the restaurant door, and pulled out my chair. My ex-husband had never done any of that.

Over dinner he was up front about having been in prison for armed robbery, and explained that it had all been a mistake—he hadn't been anywhere near the robbery. The driver of the getaway car must have been one of those identical twins we all have in the world, and the police had arrested Howard, who had been convicted.

Well, by our third date I was convinced that Howard, who was doing well in his job as a tire salesman, was a straight arrow who had paid the time for someone else's crime. It wasn't love for me, but he was a pleasant date.

When he called, on a Wednesday night, to set up our fourth date, he started the conversation by saying, "I told my brother that you and I are getting married, and he was real happy for me."

I stopped washing dishes and said, "Run that by me again," which he did.

I said, "Listen, Howard, we've had one dinner and been to two movies, and I don't think that means we're engaged. Besides, I just got dumped from a seven-year marriage, so I'm in no rush. Do you understand? It's nothing personal."

There was a long pause, and he said, "I would never be interested in a woman who was chasing me down for a wedding ring. That's why I know you and I'll be getting married soon. Don't worry about a thing. I'll pick you up Saturday at seven. Bye, sweetheart."

Sweetheart? Yuck. What happened? What was it about me that made the only two guys I ever dated start hearing wedding bells?

I decided to put the brakes on our sudden race to the altar, and called him a few hours later. I left a message on his ma-

chine saying that I had a relative staying with me that weekend, and so couldn't go out. I added that I wanted to set up
a date for the following Saturday. The point was that I wanted
to see him, but not for the rest of my life. I felt pretty good
about how I handled that.

When I hadn't heard from him by Friday morning, I assumed he was upset about my cancellation, and I planned to
call him at lunchtime. As I got out of my car at work, I saw a
black blotch moving along the edge of the parking lot. I
cleaned my sunglasses, then put them back on. Nothing there.
I needed one more cup of coffee to be fully awake, anyway.

There it was again—a blur. And again.

Was it Howard, darting from tree to tree?

I waved and yelled, "Howard! Is that you?" But nothing
moved, and I chalked up the blur to reflections and glares.

At lunch, I left a message for Howard at his job and went
next door to the deli to get a sandwich. The line was long, and
I turned to the entrance to see if my girlfriend had shown up,
and there was the blur again, dropping behind the picture
window. I would have to go in for a glaucoma test.

That night, unloading groceries from my car, the blur
moved from bush to bush in my neighbor's yard across the
street. I stood still, wondering if I should check it out, and
thought better of it.

I met a girlfriend for dinner, and just as we were about to
dive into our pizza, I heard my name come over the public address system. A call for me? I put the receiver to my ear.

"It's Howard, sweetie. How's the pizza? When is your relative coming in town? You look great in that pink sweater."

I looked around. Where was he that he could even see
what I was wearing?

"Are you spying on me, Howard?" I asked, irritated.

"Don't be paranoid. I just guessed. Gotta go. I want five
groomsmen, so pick five of your male relatives. Bye."

In the next week, he left notes on my windshield, had me

paged at supermarkets, and called me at a work party that was held on the outskirts of town at a country club.

There was no doubt that he was following me. The other odd thing was, he wasn't calling to set up dates, just to let me know that he was keeping tabs on me. It was harmless, but bothersome stuff.

Two weeks later, at the office, I was lost in thought. I sat in the back of a room that was divided into about twenty cubicles. I heard gasps come from the front of the area, then titters, then a scream—which is when I finally looked up from my work and leaned over to glance down the aisle.

Was it a Navy Seal? There was a guy in tight black clothes, black gloves, his face painted black, crawling on his stomach up the aisle.

"Howard?" I asked, shocked. He locked eyes with me and continued his steady crawl.

Secretaries were on their feet, screaming, as two security guards hauled Howard to his feet.

At the security station, Howard told me, the security team, my boss, and the president of the company that he had just wanted to see if his fiancée—me—was talking to any men at work. This was a prime concern, he said, since I had been moody since our engagement. He said he never planned on harming anyone.

Strangely enough, the company didn't press charges. The next morning, my boss told me, "We think you should take the next couple of months off, reorganize your life, get some issues straightened out. When you're ready to come back, give us a call and we'll see what we can do."

I could have protested, maybe hired an attorney to make my company maintain my job, but frankly, the thought of having to bear the embarrassment of returning to work was too much for me. That morning had been terrible. I said, "Throw in some heavy-duty severance pay and medical benefits and you've got yourself a deal."

I cleared out my desk and went home. That night, at four

in the morning, I woke up and screamed. Howard was sitting in a rocking chair beside my bed, smiling and staring at me.

"I just wanted to see how beautiful you look when you're asleep," he said.

When I asked how long he'd been there and how'd he gotten in, he said, "Coupla hours. Helped myself to a soda and a sandwich—hope you don't mind. Picked the lock. Gotta go now. Bye, honey."

I called the police, but Howard had left.

After the second time I awoke to find Howard in my rocking chair, I sneaked another call to the police, who came over and arrested him.

Howard was back on the street the next day, and broke into my house three more times before he was arrested again. The police told me that they had just learned that I was the fifth woman that Howard had followed since he'd gotten out of prison. Howard didn't date women, he stalked them. I had been dating a stalker. Just my luck.

After three months, he was released on parole and never came back. Two days later, he was arrested for robbing a jewelry store at gunpoint. He'd been loading his bag with engagement rings.

My girlfriend said, "That's so sad. He was sent back to prison for loving you. Poor thing. Listen, I know this other guy who's available. He's got tattoos on his neck and arms, I think, but it might not be a bad place to start, you know, to put Howard behind you. What do you think?"

For a split second, I actually thought it over.

—Audrey, 29, nutritionist, South Dakota

✳   ✳   ✳

8

* * * *

Getting Even

It's payback time. They just plain had it coming—right? Don't gloat—every so often, the retaliation is directed right at *you*. There's still nothing as sweet as old-fashioned revenge.

ivil court—I was being sued in civil court because of a bad date? The Manhattan judge ordered me to pay the claimant, a.k.a. my date, $161.46 including filing fees and interest. I couldn't believe it.

My date, whom we'll call Linda, claimed that I had committed a breech of contract where our date was concerned, and that I owed her half the value of the date.

Here's my side of what happened.

Linda and I met through mutual friends at an outdoor jazz concert in New York City. During our conversation, we talked about how she was in sales and I was in law school. She mentioned that she wanted to take a trip to Nantucket Island.

Later Linda told me she was making plans to go to Nantucket for a weekend, and asked if I wanted to come along. It sounded like a very casual trip, and I agreed.

Linda and I took a train from Manhattan to Connecticut.

There Linda used her credit card to rent a car, and we drove to Hyannis Port. I insisted we go Dutch treat. She agreed, and I paid her for my half of the rental car in cash.

She had selected our bed-and-breakfast on Nantucket. We had agreed to share a room to keep down costs. On the island, we were shown to our room. It had a big canopy bed that implied "for lovers." I whispered to the innkeeper, "Can you get us a room with two single beds right away?"

The innkeeper obliged, announcing, "My mistake. This is the wrong room," and showed us to a room with two single beds.

Linda became upset, telling the innkeeper that this was not the kind of room she had wanted.

By that point I had become increasingly skittish around Linda. It bothered me that she was so controlling. It was definitely best to be firm about a just-friends course.

The first night, after I had gotten into my bed, she jumped on top of me, knocking the wind out of me, and said, "Well, you got me here to have sex, didn't you?"

Staying calm, I nonchalantly said, "No. I'm tired. Good night." I yanked on the sheets until I could pull them up to my face and I twisted away from her.

She made a noise of disgust, then got off me.

The next morning we went to a little restaurant for breakfast. When our food arrived, Linda looked at hers and said, "I didn't order scrambled eggs and hash."

I told her that I thought she had, and she jumped onto our table and ranted, "Why doesn't anyone ever listen to me? I didn't order scrambled eggs and hash!"

Everyone was watching and listening, and I was stunned.

As calmly as I could, I said, "Linda, come down off the table." I took her hand and firmly said, "Linda, come down."

She took my hand and sat in her chair, staring at me. I made small talk for a while, then said, "You know, you're obviously under a lot of stress. You probably need some time alone so you can relax. Let's spend the day apart. We can rent bicycles and go our separate ways, and meet back at the inn at seven tonight for dinner. Then we can tell each other what we did."

She was glum and angry, but she agreed.

At seven that night, as I was riding back to our inn, it was dark and chilly. When I got to our room, without turning the light on I went to the walk-in closet and reached for my sweater. As I reached in, something latched onto my arm, and I jumped out of my skin.

A voice said, "I've been waiting for you."

I looked down and there was Linda, sitting in a child's rocking chair that she had dragged into the closet.

I was in a horror movie. The gleam in her eyes made me shiver.

I recovered, trying not to look terrified. Swallowing, I said, "I'm so glad to see you. Are you ready to go?"

Puzzled, she stared at me, then let go of my arm and followed me out of the room.

At dinner, Linda railed about how badly men behaved in relationships. When she got louder, I told her I would only stay if she behaved.

After dinner, we went to a bar where there was dancing, and Linda had at least three drinks. People were dancing as a group, and I joined in, yelling for her to dance, too. She left, and I danced two more songs.

At the inn, she said, "What about—"

And I cut her off, anticipating her bid at sex, and I said, "No."

She looked frazzled and I explained, "I don't want this. I don't want you the way you want me. We're friends."

I thought I'd diffused the situation. But the next morning, she looked furious. While we were bike riding, I stopped to take a photo of a house, and she kept going. When I got back on my bike, she was blocks away, and I made a U-turn, spending the rest of the day alone.

I didn't sit with her on the train, and I didn't hear from her for a week. Then she started calling me at work. I was clerking for a judge, and she started leaving messages with the secretary saying I had raped her. She told the law school guards the same story. She called me at home. She began stalking me, appearing behind me from time to time. I had her calls blocked at work and told the doormen at my apartment building not to let her in.

Two weeks later she called me at home and said, "If you don't see me tomorrow, I'm suing you."

It was a hollow threat, I thought, and ignored her.

Three days later, a summons arrived for me. She was suing. Linda claimed I had committed a breach of contract where our date was concerned, and that I owed her half the value of the date.

In fact, only two transactions from our trip were made with a credit card—which produced valid receipts—and in each case it was with Linda's; the rental car and one meal. Both times I had reimbursed her for my half in cash.

But in court, Linda came up with other cash receipts that she had been collecting on our trip—receipts for bills we always split evenly. I had assumed she was collecting them as some sort of tax deduction. In court she told the judge that since she had all the receipts, she had proof that she had paid for everything.

Linda portrayed me as a cheapskate who hadn't paid for anything. While our hearing was progressing, I could see in the female judge's face that I was doomed. But with no real evidence and no witnesses, I expected the judge to dismiss the case as frivolous. I was a law student, after all, and could recognize an unsubstantial case.

The trial lasted forty minutes before the judge issued her decision: I lost. Later the judge told a newspaper that she "might have identified with the claimant."

"I'm innocent," I said, even as the case made the newspapers.

Why would Linda take me to court? I can only chalk it up

to revenge. I was the first date Linda had had in ages, and when it became clear that I wasn't head-over-heels about her, she sued.

I already had an MBA, and I was so disillusioned with the courts that I didn't finish law school.

The case lasted two years. In that time, I made an ethics complaint about the judge for letting her personal feelings enter her decision. I appealed the case, and it went through a total of three levels of the court system, but was not overturned.

So here's the bottom line: You can be sued as easily as I was for being a bad date. If you don't draw up a pre-datal contract, at least keep your receipts. That's your only proof. Even if the date is Dutch.

—Louis, 35, international marketing, New York City

✳ ✳ ✳

Three days earlier, I had been promoted over a colleague and she had been looking homicidal ever since. We had hated each other since the day we met. I had pulled off this promotion by not passing on pertinent information I was supposed to share with her (one of *her* typical ploys). But she didn't know that.

She congratulated me, and we started talking. She was actually pleasant. Then she said, "Are you still looking for a date for that charity dance? I have a great guy for you. He's an old friend." According to her, he was handsome, smart, successful, and funny. I told her I'd think about it. A week later, with no date on the horizon, I told her I'd take her up on her offer, and she happily said she'd take care of it.

Her friend, Blake, called and sounded terrific. Maybe my colleague had a sweet side after all.

The night of the dance, Blake was a dream date. In fact, he was the best date I had had in ages.

After the dance, not wanting the evening to end, we went out for a late, light supper.

When we were seated he actually read the wine list, rather than skim the prices for a steal. Then he spoke with the sommelier, asking his advice on the two wines he'd narrowed it down to.

He made a selection, grinned at me, and said, "I think you're going to like this wine. It's one of my favorites," and I smiled back. This was wonderful!

After two glasses of delicious wine, I couldn't have cared less what I ate, and asked him to order for me.

Our appetizers arrived, and I was transported. For himself, he'd ordered grilled mushrooms, and for me, mussels.

I loved the mussels, and told him so.

He said, "I'm glad. Try mine," and I choked.

He had a mouthful of food, and while he was talking, he'd shown it all to me. He smacked his lips and made odd slurping noises.

Even so, I decided that one or two bad eating habits weren't all there was to an otherwise perfect guy. Other than talking with food in his mouth, I liked him.

I said, "I can't wait for my entrée."

He opened his mouth to talk to me, and I noticed that he had a golf ball lodged in his cheek. I realized that that's where he had stored a wad of food so that he could answer me. The second he stopped talking, he spooned in more food, showed it to me while he talked, then decided to swallow the stored-up portion.

My stomach turned. But I could take this. Once we'd settled into a long-term relationship, I'd be able to toss some subtle hints his way to straighten up his dinner table act. I tried one out.

"We don't have to talk till we're through eating," I said.

He forked the last huge mushroom on his plate, stuffed it in his mouth, using the fingers on his left hand to fold in any overhang, and said, while chewing this blob, "No problem! I'm finished! How about you?"

I swallowed the urge to say, "Stop that right now!" and instead stared at my mussels, feeling queasy.

At that moment, I could almost hear my colleague at work whisper, "Gotcha." There was no way she couldn't have known about Blake's eating habits, and there was no way she wouldn't have found out by now that I'd shafted her at work. We were definitely even now. I hated her more than ever.

I composed myself, telling myself that aside from making me sick to my stomach, Blake was an okay guy. If we kept dating, we would just have separate meals.

I looked up at him, but he was a little blurry.

I took off my glasses and looked at them, and said, "What's this? There's some goo on my glasses," and started to wipe them with my napkin.

"Oh," he said, noisily slurping his wine, "that's probably mushrooms."

"What?" I asked.

Just then something flew toward my eyes, lodging on my eyelashes.

When he talked, he spewed his food, and was splattering me.

I said, "Check!"

This dinner was on me.

—Cynthia, 29, game designer, North Carolina

* * *

S itting in the driveway with a jumbo bag of Oreo cookies, I reflected on my situation. My girlfriend was in bed, in her house, with one of my friends. How I knew this fact wasn't interesting. What was more intriguing was how I was going to handle it.

I had popped over to share a midnight snack of cookies but

instead wound up ruminating on a plan. Did I want to yell at them, stay calm and guilt-trip them, act like I didn't know and had started to date someone else, or murder him and wound her?

I rested my head against a tire of her car, twisting apart another Oreo, not actually deep in thought, mostly numb.

I pulled up the collar of my jacket and heard a scraping sound. A button of my jacket had skimmed the side of her car—her new car. Her new, three-day-old, shiny red BMW that she babied, pampered, loved. Loved more than me, that much was sure.

I stood up, contemplating kicking the life out of the tires, scraping the sides of the car with a key. I unscrewed another Oreo, popped the cookie side into my mouth, and stuck the cookie-and-creme side to the windshield. Looked pretty good. So I stuck on another one.

A half-hour later, I stepped back to survey my handiwork. I had Oreo'ed the entire car—even part of the roof. It looked great.

She would have a fit, I knew, and it would take a while to get the smeary creme off the car, especially after it had set all night, hopefully holding like glue.

I went home and came back with a camera. The Oreo'ed car was a beauty, and the details showed up well in pictures. I mailed a copy of the photo to her later, and I really did feel better.

—Mark, 26, sculptor, Miami

* * *

The scumbag had been dating me and my younger sister at the same time. My sister, Nicole, and I found out by accident. She'd been describing her third date with a guy named Paul who sounded an awful lot like a guy I'd been dating for two months named Arnie.

Nicole and I pieced it together. She and I looked almost identical, and we'd each told him in great detail about our family. He'd started dating her not long after I told him that she was a personal trainer at the new health club.

We decided to get even.

Arnie and I had a date Friday night, and he and Nicole had a date Saturday. I told him I'd meet him at his place Friday night. To get him primed, I told him not to count on going to dinner or to a movie, that I'd be his entertainment.

He said, "I like the sound of that! Don't be late!"

I was on time, with Nicole in tow.

When Arnie opened his door, his smile crumbled into shock, then fear, when he saw that we were together.

I said, "Don't say anything. We figured it out, and we're not mad. Can we come in?"

We went straight to his bedroom and sat on the bed.

Nicole said, "You like dating sisters, don't you?"

Arnie, still in shock, let one ray of titillation brighten his face. He nodded, then shook his head, then gave a little shrug.

I said, "How would you like to sleep with both of us?"

His mouth fell open, and his tongue was hanging out. Neither Nicole nor I had slept with him, so this was a double enticement to Arnie.

In answer, he flung himself on his bed.

Nicole said, "My sister and I are into kinky stuff. Are you?"

Arnie was breathing heavily, and gulped, "I don't know. Let's try. I'm glad you're not mad. I like you both."

To lure him into dropping his defenses, we undressed down to our camisoles and tap pants, then pulled off Arnie's shirt and pants, leaving him in his boxer shorts.

I opened his sock drawer, pulled out a few pair, and said, "You're in our control now."

Nicole and I flipped him onto his stomach and used the socks to tie him spread-eagled to the bedposts.

Arnie twisted his head around to us and said, "This is gonna be different."

I said, "Yes."

We turned on the TV in the bedroom to full volume, then turned his stereo to a hard rock station.

Nicole and I got dressed and stood over Arnie, and I said, "I guess this is a good time to tell you that we're mad at you for being a two-timer. Good luck with those knots."

We left the room, closing the door behind us, hearing Arnie's parting words: "One thing: What exactly are you mad about?"

—Parvine, 20, waitress, Trenton, New Jersey

✳ ✳ ✳

Religious differences? Political enmity? No. Stuart just bugged me, that's all. He irritated and bored me. At first I'd liked him, but he was the kind of guy who the more you knew about him, the less you liked. So after five months of dating, I broke it off with him.

A few days later, Stuart called and said, "Do me one last favor. I'm throwing that big gala party thing in two weeks. All my friends are gonna be looking for you. I'll need a date, and I don't want to throw a damper on the evening having to explain that we broke up, so why don't you come? I won't bother you, and you'll have a great time—you ought to, anyway. You picked the place and the caterers and the champagne. What do you say?"

I said, "I'd love to!" I felt like it was my party, and wanted to see how it would turn out. It was his fortieth birthday party, and it was deluxe.

The room looked spectacular, and I found the table that held my place card and sat down. The table sat six. Strangely, all six of us were women. We all had a nice time. Right before our entrées arrived, the woman to my left said, "Stuart is so cute. I think he seated me here so that no one else could get to me."

I said, "Why would he do that?" and she said, "Oh, we've been dating for a couple of months. He's just very proprietary. How do you know Stuart?"

I skirted the question and asked for more details of their dating life.

The woman to my right said, "Excuse me. I don't mean to eavesdrop. But is one of you dating Stuart? Because *I'm* the one dating Stuart."

"What?" inquired the woman across from me. "I've been going out with Stuart for three months."

All five of the women were involved with Stuart, including the twenty-three-year-old he had met earlier in the week. They turned to me and said, "What about you?"

I said, "I was dating him, but I broke up with him a couple of weeks ago."

For thirty seconds there was stunned silence, until a collective rage built. Like them, I was livid. He had been hinting toward marriage, which was what motivated me to end things. And the whole time, he'd been seeing five other women.

This explained my situation. Stuart had invited me so that I could see that he wasn't crushed by me. As for the others, I think he invited them so that he could look like a stud to his friends and colleagues on his fortieth birthday. I hoped everyone realized what a jerk he was.

But he got his revenge on me, all right. I couldn't believe how suddenly jealous I felt. All the women at the table were smart, pleasant, and pretty. And I had felt that Stuart was lucky to have gone out with me.

He actually stopped by the table and said, "Good evening, ladies. You all look beautiful. Can I get a picture with you?" Before anyone could protest, a bulb flashed.

I had a copy of that picture. It showed Stuart beaming as six women looked like they wanted to take him apart limb by limb. There was also the oncoming spray of champagne from a bottle that the furious twenty-three-year-old had shaken and pointed his way. Stuart looked happy as a clam.

—Esther, 42, textile designer, Dallas

* * *

A baby roach could make her queasy. Honeybees incited her to run in circles, screaming. Worms in the soil she was gardening made her nauseous.

So when she dumped me on a Thursday night and started dating my roommate on Friday night, I remembered those delicate reactions of hers that I had once found charming and feminine and endearing. Now they just made her ripe for revenge.

Friday night, around midnight, I let myself into her house and waited in her bedroom.

I heard my roommate's car pull into her driveway. As his car pulled away, I emptied my sack onto her bed and under her pillows, then pulled the covers up, tucking the bedspread nicely under the pillows, and left.

I waited outside, feeling guilty, and decided to knock and tell her what I'd done, and right my wrong.

Just as I had my hand up to knock, I heard her screams. My second thoughts were too little too late. She'd climbed into bed, probably, and found the eight or so tarantulas I'd put there.

My last thought, as I walked away feeling empty instead of elated, was that I hoped she hadn't sat on one and killed it. Tarantulas are basically friendly creatures once you get to know them.

—John, 26, sportswriter, Oklahoma

* * *

f it was a brush-off, I sure wasn't getting the hint in a big way.

At first, Dan would cancel our Saturday night plans four days in advance, switching our date to a Thursday or Wednesday night, because: (a) he had a company party he had to go to; (b) he was going out of town; or, (c) his parents were visiting all weekend. I finally caught on when he said he was canceling because: (d) he was going to work the whole weekend. Sure. First of all, no one ever does that. Second, that's the oldest excuse in the book.

Since we had friends in common, I knew he wasn't juggling me around because he was gay or married. That left one conclusion: He was seeing at least one woman besides me.

On a Tuesday night, after going back to Dan's place after dinner, we went straight to his little kitchen to get some water. I saw that his answering machine said that five calls had come in.

"Aren't you going to check your calls? I'd be dying to," I said.

Dan acted nonchalant and said, "No. It's probably work stuff. Follow me," and winked as he went to the bedroom.

I leaned on the kitchen counter, staring at the answering machine, wondering who the calls were from. I ran my finger across the edge of the machine, speculating on how many were from a woman, or from more than one woman.

I lifted the lid on the machine, checking how much tape had been used. Plenty. I stared at the take-up spool, wondering what long-winded love message was sitting there ready to be listened to, while I was in bed with what was probably a real creep.

Then I saw it. The key to his machine. There, in boldface, were the numbers 1-2-3. That was the check-in code. When Dan was away from home, he could call his own phone number, punch in that 1-2-3 code, and check his calls. Voilà.

If he hadn't bothered to change his code, all that anyone— like me—needed to check his calls was this simple code.

I wasn't sure that I could go through with eavesdropping on his machine. But later that week, he called to cancel our Friday night plans, saying, "I have to entertain an out-of-town client for work. He's some suit from London. How about next Monday night instead?"

I merrily said, "Sure! No problem! Sounds great! See you then!"

Then I waited. I waited until the next day, then I nervously dialed his number around six o'clock, punched in his code, and held my breath.

Yes! It worked. The electronic voice said, "You have three messages," and proceeded to relay them. Two from male buddies, one from the electric company saying that he was behind on his bill.

I was deflated. Maybe Dan was telling the truth after all. The next day, Friday, I checked again. There it was.

"Hi! It's Kimberly! I tried calling you at work, but no one answered. I was wondering if we can make it at nine instead of eight Friday night. Here's the address of the restaurant—I'll meet you there, okay? Call me! Bye!"

Bye! I crumpled up the restaurant information I'd scribbled down. The scumbag had a date. I'd give him one last chance. I called him at work to see if his plans had fallen through. Dan responded, "I wish! I've got to have dinner with a corporate bore with a British accent who thinks bonds are a blast. Pity me."

I said, "I will! Bye!"

At nine-fifteen, I entered the restaurant, saw Dan and his date, and marched past the maître d' to their table.

"Hi, Kimberly," I said, watching Dan's face freeze when he looked at me. "Hi, Dan. I guess you could make it at nine instead of eight after all. That's great for you, Kimberly, isn't it? And the electric company called again and said to pay your bill. Your mother wants to know why you aren't meeting them in Miami next month. The fourth message is from me telling you that I hope you pass your venereal disease on to Kimberly so I won't be the only one who has it."

Dan, never a bright light, clearly wasn't absorbing the whole situation. I summed it up for him: "Don't call me. I'll call you." Actually, I meant that I'd call his answering machine.

All he said was, "How did you know we'd be here? How do you know all these things?"

I'd been deceived by a dope.

I checked his machine periodically for a couple of months more, just out of habit, and because I couldn't believe he wasn't falling for the persuasive guilt trip his mother was giving him, and because I loved the way Kimberly said—several times—"Stop calling me. Just stop. No matter what you say, I'll never believe that you aren't infected. She seemed like a really nice girl, and I don't want to be in her shoes. It's gross. So leave me alone."

Who says revenge isn't sweet? The perfect kind, I tell my girlfriends, is as easy as 1-2-3.

—Lisa, 33, oral surgeon, Minneapolis

9

* * * *

You Should Have Known Better

Aren't your instincts screaming? Isn't your guardian angel tapping your shoulder? Isn't your higher self pleading with you? And what do you do? Ignore them all ...

Max was adorable, but I found that my nerves were often short with him. For instance, the first morning after we slept together, I watched him leave for work. Since my apartment was directly across from the elevators, I kept my door open about a foot and beamed at him. Max stood in front of the bank of elevators, beaming back at me, returning twice for kisses.

I said, "I think it'll help if you push the down button."

He said, "Oh!" smiling at me, and pushed the button. "My mind is elsewhere," he explained, making my heart skip.

The light went off on the elevator button.

I said, "Get ready. It's coming, and the doors open and close quickly."

I heard the "ding," and saw the far left door open. Max sauntered toward the open elevator, and before he was even halfway there, the doors shut. He turned to smile at me, then leisurely walked to me and gave me a long kiss before turning the face the elevators.

"Better push the button again," I said, smiling happily.

"Oh," he said, reaching for the down button.

"You have to hurry," I said cheerfully.

The light went off and I said, "Get ready!"

There was the ding, and my head swiveled to the right where a set of elevator doors opened.

I said, pointing to the right, "It's that one! Bye!"

Max looked left, then right, took three steps, and the doors closed.

I'd lived in the building three years and never once had a problem getting in the elevator. This was strange.

He shrugged, smiled at me, and gave me another kiss. This time, I wasn't interested in the kiss. I was gritting my teeth and having flashbacks.

Last night was the first time Max had driven. Before, we'd met after work at restaurants near our offices. But last night he had picked me up at my apartment and driven.

On the highway, going about fifty miles an hour in the fast lane, Max had suddenly downshifted from fourth gear to third, making the car lurch. I kept waiting for him to correct the situation, but it wasn't until I yelled over the roar, "You can blow the engine this way. Shift to fourth!" that he did. This happened one more time, lunging me toward the windshield.

Then, after we'd pulled into the parking lot, crawling at about two miles an hour, Max saw an empty parking space up ahead and put on his blinker. That was cute, I thought. But then he came to a complete stop, and eyed the space, his blinker tick-tocking. Max scanned the pavement ahead. I got annoyed. What was he waiting for? There was no one behind us, and certainly no oncoming traffic.

"All clear!" I had chirped, wanting to scream, "Just get in the space!"

He pulled in, but since the wheels hadn't made a full turn, the blinker continued to tick. Rather than turn off the engine, he thumbed through his wallet, reached into the back seat for his jacket, and opened the glove compartment for a stick of gum. The blinker was ticking the whole time.

Finally, I said, "Your blinker is on. You forgot to turn off your blinker."

Max turned off the engine and opened his door.

I said, "Your lights are on."

He got out of the car, and I did, too, to yell over the roof, *"You forgot to turn off the lights!"*

"Oh!" he'd said.

My hands were balled into fists at my side, my neck was ramrod straight, my jaw was jutting out, and my teeth were clenched. I bit back the urge to say, "Fix the blinker so it won't start up again when you turn the ignition," but I let it slide and took deep breaths.

Dinner had been pleasant. Max was great company. But on the way to my place, I realized that after he had come to a full stop, he would start moving while still in fourth gear, making the car gurgle and shudder, nearly stalling. Twice he slowed to a crawl when a traffic light was green, in anticipation of it turning orange.

He also had a tendency to hit the brakes from time to time for no reason, slinging my head toward the dashboard. Once, so exasperated that I couldn't contain myself, I'd said, "Why are you doing that?"

Max calmly answered, "Because the car up ahead put on its brake lights. I like to drive defensively."

I had scanned the horizon, spotted two small red bees, and said, "That car is about two miles ahead of us, climbing a hill," and he'd nodded, pleased.

By the time we'd gotten to my place, I was out of the car before Max had come to a complete stop in the parking space, his blinker flashing the entire time.

He was irritating, and too exasperating for me. We were not a good match, and if I were subjected to one more manifestation of his absentmindedness, I would scream. The reasonable conclusion was to part company as nicely as possible, and as soon as possible. I would definitely not invite him up for a drink. Why spend any more time with a guy who was driving me nuts? That was the sensible response, and I'd have been proud of myself in the morning.

But Max was so sweet, so handsome, so smart, that I'd told myself, "You're just being a Type A. What's a little bad driving? You're going to write him off because he's a lousy driver? Look at the big picture. Ask him up."

So there we were the next morning, at the elevators. I was wondering if I should put my robe on so I could hold the elevator door open long enough for Max to saunter on board.

The words tumbled out. I said, "Don't you live in an elevator building? Do you miss a lot of elevators? How do you get to work in the morning?"

"Who, me?" he asked, and I felt my blood pressure rise again. "Oh. Well, usually someone else on my floor shows up to go to work, too, and then I get on."

"So you do it together? It takes two—you and anyone else who happens to be going to work at the same time?"

Max thought about it, smiled, and said, "I guess!"

I sighed and said, "You need to press the down button." I waved goodbye to him, closed my door, and groaned.

I heard a ding, and through the peephole I saw him wait three full seconds to respond, long enough to miss the elevator. I grabbed my robe, flung open my door, thinking, "*This* is how you do it," and pressed the button.

When the light went off, I listened for the ding, darted to the door, and held it open.

I motioned in a circle, like a school crossing guard. The elevator was packed, and because I was embarrassed, I sounded a little harsh. I said, "Come on, come on. Over here."

Max loped on, standing right on the threshold, which made me grimace, and said, "I had a great time. Will I see you later?"

I wanted to cry. How could I tell him that if I saw him

again I'd just want to shoot myself? That the way he got from place to place made me want to scream?

I stepped back, and the doors sandwiched his shoulders, pulled back, sandwiched him again, pulled back, and a hand held the door open. Someone said, "You have to step all the way in." And I heard my date say, "Oh!"

—Natalie, 29, advertising executive, Cleveland.

✳ ✳ ✳

Forced to describe his personality, I suppose the only word that comes to mind is *creep*.

He was a blind date, introduced by normally intelligent, sensitive, perceptive mutual friends.

My date sat across from me at dinner, and the only time I heard him speak was to the waiter to place his order. Otherwise, he looked at his plate, around the restaurant, at patrons at other tables, but never at me. It was as if he were serenely dining alone.

I have no idea why I sat past our first silent glass of wine. I was doing all the talking. A dating patron saint whispered to me, "Get your purse and leave. It only gets worse."

Instead, I held on to a friendly manner, occasionally making some remarks, mostly making sure that dinner progressed as quickly as possible. I was not going to provide an awkward situation for our mutual friends by ending early. I would stick this out.

Foolishly having ordered dessert, I excused myself.

In the ladies' room, my reason returned, and I slung my purse strap over my neck and stood on the toilet seat, trying to reach the window. No luck.

I chugged my coffee, wolfed down my crème brûlée, and pantomimed to the waiter that I wanted our check, hoping I also telegraphed, from desperate facial expressions, to step on it.

To expedite the closing of our evening, the second the waiter appeared with our bill, I didn't give him time to put it on the table. I handed the waiter my charge card and said, "I'm in a huge hurry."

I was signing the bill, tearing off my copy, when my date spoke to me. He said, "I know everything about you. I looked you up in *Who's Who*."

I stopped in the middle of opening my handbag, looked at him, and said, "Really. Ready to go?"

Outside, I shook his hand and race-walked to my car.

The next day, a manila envelope arrived at my office. Inside was a photocopy of a *Who's Who* entry on my date from last night.

A yellow note was stuck to the photocopy. In true laconic form, the note had no greeting and closing. It had two words: "We're even."

What a secure man—and what a charmer.

—Andrea, 34, urban planner, Austin

* * *

Australia was gorgeous—particularly Australian men.

Experience had taught me that it was nearly impossible to get something going with a foreign man while I was on a trip—especially when I had a new destination every day. But my mind was lagging behind that day.

I was traveling with a group of girlfriends, and we stopped at a farm that was on our tour map.

There was one guy in particular whom I fell for instantly. Tall, tan, lean, wicked smile. He was conducting the tour and stared at me the entire time. Even though we were all in our early thirties, my friends were giggling and teasing me.

It was an all-day tour, and we were exhausted. I checked my watch. Six o'clock. Time had run out to make any contact with my dream man. At least we'd been flirting and smiling at each other—at least, I had been.

As the group was making its way to the last stop of the farm tour, he fell back to walk with me and said, "Would you like to go out tonight? You can bring your friends, if you like."

I could only nod, hoping I wasn't blushing. This was turning out to be the best ending to the day that I could have imagined.

We all took our seats in the makeshift stands as my Aussie and two other men led in seven cows and tethered them to a wall. This was preparation for the milking demonstration.

My Aussie started plucking people from the audience, then stalled on the seventh pick, finally grinning largely and pointing to me. When I passed him, he said, "I gave you my favorite. She's a sweetheart."

I got down to my cow and took a step back. This was not like any cow I'd ever seen, and I'd seen a lot of cows. She was the size of a cargo carrier.

I took my seat on the little stool, and listened while someone gave us instructions.

Sounded simple.

I looked underneath my cow for the described anatomy and felt miffed. My cow had twenty-four udders if it had two.

Pull and squeeze, pull and squeeze were the instructions. I took hold of one udder and pulled, and smiled into the camera as one of my friends pointed it in my direction. I grabbed a second udder, and noticed that my Aussie was beaming me with the most angelic, sexy, appreciative smile I'd ever seen. I was so busy looking at him, I didn't know what happened next.

All I knew was that I was lying flat on my ass, clouds of dirt billowing around me, and my thigh was killing me.

My cow had kicked me. I had either done something wrong and accidentally hurt her, or our milking instructions had been lame.

I heard rhythmic sounds, like squirt-squirt, and saw that the six milkers were contentedly leaning their heads against their cows' bellies, milking away. They looked like six experienced, serene milkmaids.

My Aussie gave me a disbelieving look and helped me to my feet. But he wasn't looking at me. His gaze had locked with the stare of the blonde from Florida who had been milking to my right. Her movements were fluid and steady. She was so darn good at it, I expected her to start milking with one hand tied behind her back, or to tie on a blindfold. She was the one who captured my Aussie's heart.

When they walked off together after the demonstration, I wasn't surprised, but I wasn't happy. Nor was I happy when my girlfriend showed me an out-of-focus Polaroid of me on my ass, my feet in the air.

"Here's one for the scrapbook!" my friend said.

She was right. In the background of the photo, clearly visible and in perfect focus, was the Aussie-stealing Florida milker, smiling and milking away.

—Rebecca, 33, surgeon, Oregon

* * *

Traffic court—jammed, crowded, guaranteed to be expensive—was the last place I expected to be as a consequence of a date. But there I was, complaining to the judge.

The aforementioned date's name was Lyle. We'd had a terrific first date, then I didn't hear from him for a week. He called with an excellent alibi: He'd twisted his ankle while stepping off a curb, spraining it so badly that it was in a cast, and he was on pain medication.

Over the phone he said, "I wish I could take you out to dinner, but I'm really laid up. I'll call you when I'm back on my feet."

I said, "Why don't I drive over to your place and fix us dinner?"

Lyle said, "Really? What a great idea! You'd do that? I hadn't thought of that, but I'd love it. If you're sure you don't mind, let's do it!"

I bought swordfish, which I marinated in lime juice and cilantro. I prepared a wild rice dish with yellow raisins and pecans. I bought baby salad greens and made a balsamic vinaigrette. For appetizers, I went to my favorite gourmet store and got French goat cheese and a nice baguette. Then I bought a chocolate mousse cake, and splurged on a really nice bottle of wine. In short, I spent a small fortune on dinner.

When I pulled in front of his house, Lyle was waiting on his porch for me.

"Don't park there!" he said. "You might get a ticket. Park over there."

I didn't see any signs that indicated that I was in the wrong place. And frankly, the sign at the space that Lyle was pointing to had ambiguous restrictions. I should have remained parked where I was, trusting my deductions, but Lyle was persistent and I didn't want to seem hardheaded, so I moved to his spot.

I set about getting dinner ready. Lyle asked what we were having, and I said, "A feast for a king. I pulled out all the stops."

I showed him the ingredients, and I waited for him to say, "Let me chip in on the cost." That would have been the appropriate time for him to offer, and it would have been right for me to say, "Absolutely not," so that he could say, "Next time, dinner is on me."

I smiled and waited for this exchange to get going.

He said, "Great!"

That should have been my first clue to his character. I might as well have been showing him peanut butter and jelly. All that mattered to him was that he was being fed—by someone else. I shrugged it off.

We ate. I waited for praise. As if on cue, he said, "Doesn't swordfish have mercury in it? I'll pass and just eat this other stuff."

Otherwise, dinner conversation was nice. Afterward we talked and finished the wine. At midnight, Lyle hobbled to my car with me.

"Oh no!" I cried, pulling two parking tickets from under a windshield wiper. "How could this happen?"

He took them out of my hand and said, "Let me take care of these. My cousin is a policeman. He'll get them torn up."

I got in my car, thrilled. Yes, I had a boyfriend now! When a guy ate your food and then got his family involved in helping you out, you were girlfriend and boyfriend.

I didn't hear from Lyle the next day, nor the next week. At the end of two weeks, I called him on the pretext of the parking tickets.

"Did you get the tickets taken care of?" I asked.

Lyle got touchy and said, "Of course I did. What do you think I am, a jerk? I said I would, and I did. My cousin fixed everything."

I asked him to send me a copy of the receipts marked "Paid," and he got huffy. When he didn't say anything else, I said goodbye. I should have called a city agency to verify that the tickets had truly been taken care of. But I felt like I was being paranoid. He wouldn't have any reason to lie, and I didn't want to spend all day getting caught up in the run-around of dealing with city government.

One month later, I received a summons in the mail for the parking tickets, totalling $150. I was livid.

I called Lyle and he said, "My cousin took care of it! Calm down. Get a grip. I did you a favor, and all you can do is get mad. Obviously it just hasn't cleared on the computer system, that's all. But I'll double-check with my cousin."

Did I call the motor vehicle department? Of course not. I was too busy, and Lyle had sounded committed.

A month later, I received another summons, along with a stern warning to pay up. With late charges, the tickets now cost $200.

I called Lyle's office and announced myself, and the secretary immediately said, "He's not available right now. But if you'd like to leave a message . . ."

So it was down to traffic court for me. I told the judge my story. ". . . so not only am I out of pocket $200 for these parking tickets, I also spent over $40 on dinner, and on our first date he bought me a hot dog at a baseball game. It was his idea I park there, not mine, and he said he'd get the tickets fixed by his cousin the cop. How do you think I feel? I feel ripped off. How was I to know that—"

The judge held up his hand and said, "Pay $100 and we'll call it even. Next."

I told my brother, whose friend set me up with Lyle, the story for the fifth time. Two days later, I received a check for $200 in the mail from Lyle along with a short apology for his "cousin's screwup." At first I didn't want to cash it, thought it would be better to mail it back to him with a nasty no-thank-you note. But I decided to deposit it, and with the extra $100, treat myself to a nice present.

A couple of days later, I came home swinging a shopping bag containing a new $100 outfit, and collected my mail.

Lyle's check to me had bounced. Not only that, but my bank was charging me a $10 penalty! I hadn't laid eyes on him in months, and somehow he was managing to make my debt get bigger and bigger.

That was an extra $110—the outfit plus the bank fee—I'd spent without even knowing it. Grand total, so far, for that date, $250, and still counting.

—Josephine, 32, nurse, Detroit

✳   ✳   ✳

Acapulco was everything I'd hoped it would be.

I'd gone with two girlfriends. Even though none of us spoke Spanish, we weren't having any trouble getting around. Most people spoke English, and the ones who didn't usually managed to help us out when we took stabs at Spanish words.

On our first night, we went to a noisy restaurant where there were a lot of Americans.

We were thrilled when a handsome Mexican man asked if he could buy us all a drink. We agreed, and invited him to sit with us.

He and I took a shine to each other, and he asked me if my friends and I liked to go dancing. He said he knew of a great club called Mi Casa.

"It's new," he said, smiling.

Against my better judgment, I said, "I'm tired of spending all my time with my friends. How about if just you and I go— and no hanky-panky." What was I saying? It wasn't ever wise to go off alone with a guy you just met, much less in a foreign country. But this seemed like an adventure to wake up my staid vacation.

He said, "*Vamos.* Let's go. I'll have you home early."

My friends were upset that I was ditching them. They wanted to come along, they said, to give me protection, and to see Acapulco through a native's eyes.

I said, "Sorry, girls! Get your own!" feeling cocky, and got into a cab with my handsome new friend.

The cab stopped in front of a residence.

I said, "Where's the club? Where's *Mi Casa?*"

He scratched his head and said, "Can your Spanish really be that bad? *Mi casa* means 'my place.' I thought everyone knew that."

I said, "I was born in Maine, but I live in Canada. I don't think we even have a Taco Bell."

I had the driver take me to my hotel, where I watched TV until my friends came in from their great night out, having gone to a real nightclub with fabulous Mexican men who had asked them out for tomorrow. Just in case I was brave enough to ask, my roommate said, "And you're not invited."

—Jewel, 30, art gallery owner, Canada

*   *   *

For weeks I'd been trying to get my nerve up to go to a nude beach.

Late on a gorgeous Saturday morning, I thought, *This is the day.* None of my friends wanted to join me, and I decided that it was probably best for me to go alone anyway. That way I wouldn't be self-conscious with a friend, I'd be anonymous.

A little voice kept telling me to wait, to try out the topless idea when I was with friends and had checked out the beach. But I was upset that my friends kept bailing out, and feeling defiant.

I walked past the clothed section at the beach and hiked up an embankment until I could go down to the protective cove where the nude sunbathers were.

I had to find the right spot—far enough away from anyone, yet close enough to the group that I wasn't isolated.

I lay down on my blanket, and took off my cutoffs, T-shirt, and sandals. I was still in my bikini. When I was through counting to five, I'd take off my suit.

On the count of three, a beach towel stretched out beside me, and a guy sat on it.

I said, "Didn't I see you watching me when I walked through that other section of the beach?"

He said, "Yeah, probably. I thought you were cute. And some buddies I didn't feel like hanging out with today showed up, so I decided to come over here. Is it all right if I join you?"

No, it wasn't all right, but I suspected that if I said no, he'd only move a couple feet away and would still try to talk to me. I didn't like him, and didn't want to talk to him, and normally

I would have said "no." But this time I was insecure, and didn't want an argument or a scene that might call attention my way, so, completely out of character, I said sure.

He talked about his job as a stereo installer for high-end sound systems, but I had my mind on other things.

I said, eyeing his T-shirt and gym shorts, "You know that you're at the nude beach, right?"

He said, "Yeah, I know."

I said, "Well, you go first."

He said, "Me? Not me!"

I was irritated, but determined not to let him spoil my plans.

I stretched out, facedown, on my blanket, and reached behind to unclasp my top and slide it off. I plastered my chest to the towel and pushed the towel against the sides of my breasts so that he couldn't see anything. I was going to have to work up the nerve to take my bottom off, because then it would be staring straight up at him, and he seemed closer than ever.

"I never take my clothes off," he said, staring at my body. "I just like to come here."

"I'm sure you do," I said.

This was not exactly freeing, lying with my chest plastered to the sand. I was talking to him with the side of my face flat against the towel. My bottom was going to stay on until he left.

After an hour of telling me why inexpensive stereos were a waste, I slid my top under my chest, tied it on, and sat up.

"Time for me to go," I said. "Nice meeting you."

He said, "Would you like to go for a drink?"

Now that I was dressed and less tense, I could see that he was okay-looking and seemed nice. I was skeptical, but I chalked those misgivings up to self-consciousness and accepted.

"Great," he said. "The only thing is, I didn't wear any shoes. But I know this little place that's ten minutes from here where they'll let us sit at a sidewalk table. I go there all the time."

As we stood up, he said, "Can you drive? I walked here."

"You walked here on a hot day without shoes?"

"Yeah, I do it all the time, so my feet are used to it."

That was odd, but I was glad to drive so I'd be in control.

At the outdoor café, we each had two drinks. At seven o'clock, I told him I had to leave, and he handed the waitress his credit card.

"We don't take plastic," the waitress said.

He told her, "This is all I have. I didn't bring any money, and you're a well-established business. I know you've taken my charge card before. This is absurd."

I said, "Don't worry. I'll pay. This has happened to me before."

He apologized profusely. On the ride to his place, he said, "I'm so embarrassed. Let me make it up to you. Let's swing by my house and I'll pick up some shoes and take you to dinner. Do you have any plans?"

I thought, *This is weird, this is how people get into trouble.* On the other hand, it was Saturday night, I was free, and I'd be driving, so it sounded good.

On the ride over to his place, he told me how he'd just bought the house. He invited me inside. It was a nice place.

He checked his answering machine, and I heard a female voice say, "You're two weeks late on the rent. Pay by Sunday night."

He said, "That's about the place I just moved out of. We're having a disagreement about the last month's rent. It's a big mess. Let's see, I've got my shoes, and I've got my bank card. Ready! Why don't you let me do the driving? You must be tired."

I didn't like the sound of that phone message, but now that I was in his house, I felt like I had to do the polite thing, and I agreed. We went to a cash machine, and then pulled up to a convenience store.

He said, "I thought I'd pick up a six-pack of beer and some sandwiches, and go back to my place and watch TV. I just got my cable hooked up, and I get fifty stations."

What? This was a horrible idea.

I said, "I have cable, too." Then I thought I'd better play along and said to get me a turkey sandwich.

When we got to his place, he walked to his front door and I walked to my car, got in, and locked the doors, fuming.

First he'd followed me to the nude beach, then wouldn't take his clothes off, which stopped me from taking off all of mine. Then I had to pay for the drinks. Then I was pretty sure I caught him in a lie, and that he was renting his house, and behind on rent. Next, he maneuvered me into his car so he could take control and head straight to a mini-grocery store. Then he planned to have me eat sandwiches and drink beer at his place. Maybe this was all about him being broke, but I was mad, not sympathetic. Was I supposed to be unaware what the next step would be? Had I been feeling so vulnerable and naive when I was topless that my reason had flown out the window, and I had been compliant—a rarity for me—when I should have been practical and assertive, and left? I was mad at myself.

He tapped on the passenger window of my car, and I lowered that window one inch, grateful I had automatic windows and door locks.

He slid his fingers into the opening and said, "What's the problem? Open the window and let's talk. What scared you? Come inside."

I had a list of things I could tell him, but instead I said, "If you ever follow me again or sit next to me at the beach or anywhere else, I'll call the police. I know where you live, and I'll send them here."

He said, "You're jumping to conclusions."

I rolled up the window tighter, but he didn't move his fingers.

I said, "Move your fingers, or I'm going to drive off anyway."

He said, "I can't. They're stuck."

I decided to take a chance. I put the car in drive, and the second I pulled away from the curb, he easily pulled his fingers away and yelled, "You'll miss me!"

The only way I would miss him was if I backed up and didn't hit him. I sped away, seeing him in the middle of the street, shoeless again, clutching his grocery bag and a six-pack.

—Bridget, 33, tax analyst, California

✳ ✳ ✳

We sat next to each other in economics class, and we were in the same study group. Her name was Roxanne, and I was crazy about her. Every guy on campus was crazy about her. I was always afraid I was going to throw myself at her and drool on her or something. I knew I had to take it slowly and earn her respect, behave with some class.

So I impressed Roxanne with my intellect and finally got up the nerve to ask, "Do you have any plans this weekend?" This was an essential warm-up question, and it provided an easy retreat.

She said, "No. Nothing. I have no plans at all."

I was completely surprised, but it was a green light, and I had to act on it before it turned red.

I said, "Why not go out for Chinese food with me Friday night?"

She smiled and accepted, and I tried not to scream.

For our dinner date, Roxanne wore a black low-cut leotard, black shorts over black biking shorts, and boots. She was a knockout.

As she got in the car, she said, "I'm so exhausted from studying. I can't believe midterms start Monday. I think I slept three hours last night from all the studying."

We had dinner, where conversation was adequate, and went to a movie, which was horrible, and she yawned and said, "Time to take me home. I've got to crash."

I had just turned the corner and her dorm was two buildings away, but Roxanne already had her hand on the door handle.

I didn't have time to put the car in park before she swung open her door, got out, said thanks, and ran up the sidewalk.

That wasn't a great date, but it wasn't as bad as some of my others. I had a suspicion that I was intentionally willing myself to overlook some vital clues, but I decided to call the next day for a follow-up call—you know, "Did you get any sleep? I had fun, did you?" This was an essential check-in call—it made you look like a gentleman and provided information, like, should you ask for a second date?

The next day, I made this call, got another green light, and asked her out for yogurt. She agreed. I almost dropped the phone.

I picked up Roxanne after she'd studied till ten, and we went to an ice cream parlor. She was quiet. I wanted to go dancing—it was Saturday night, after all. But she sighed a lot, looked at the other customers, and kept asking what time it was.

I took her home, and she did her usual rapid exit. As she got out of the car, I said, "Do you ever get out while the car is still rolling to a stop?"

She laughed, so I quickly asked, "Want to have pizza tomorrow night?"

She said, "Sure!" and ran into her dorm.

On pizza night, I tried to get a kiss *before* we got in the car to go to her dorm, but Roxanne ducked me and said, "Hey! Let's take it slow! We're both under a lot of pressure for tests."

Didn't she like me? I hunted for a clue that led me in the direction of passion and came up short, but chalked that up to getting-to-know-you jitters. She wouldn't be going out with me if she didn't like me romantically, would she?

She wasn't free on Monday, was cool as ice in class on Tuesday, and didn't return any of my calls on Wednesday. We were dating, weren't we? How else would she typify what we'd been doing?

In class Thursday, I glared and didn't say hello. She yawned all through class. Finally, at the end of the class, I said, "How are you?"

Roxanne said, "Awful."

I said, "Why?"

She said, "I was up all night making a mistake with some guy who it turns out has a girlfriend. I've had a crush on him for a year, and that's what I found out this morning. I'm exhausted."

Excuse me?

I said, "That's interesting. I thought you and I were dating."

Roxanne looked at me like she'd never seen me before, and said, "You did? Gosh. I'm in no way interested in you. I hope I'm saying that in a polite enough manner."

Oh yeah. There are so many polite ways to get that message across. And I guess I'd ignored most of them.

—Ronnie, 27, golf pro, Iowa

* * *

I loved my hippie period. I had long hair, tie-dyed shirts, bell bottoms, clogs, and an MIA bracelet. Bring back the late sixties and early seventies, please.

I came from a nice middle-class family, but I desperately wanted to be on the wrong side of the tracks for Jeremiah, a sort of tough guy with hair down to his waist who was so cool that he had his own following of friends who, like him, didn't seem to do anything for a living. I was in college, majoring in business, and didn't know how to get his complete attention.

Jeremiah mentioned that he wanted to go to Tanglewood

for a big Van Morrison concert, and I volunteered to take him in my Volkswagen van. He said we'd also be taking along two of his friends, a girl and guy who had renamed themselves Rain and Colorado.

I never had luck at outdoor concerts. Once I'd been rear-ended in the rain. Before that, coming home from a Grateful Dead concert, I must have run over a pile of nails, because I got two flat tires at once, at three in the morning. I'd given up on outdoor concerts—particularly ones I had to drive to. Experience had taught me that they were always catastrophes for me. But I tossed all my reason out the door if it meant being on a date with Jeremiah.

Between the four of us, we were rich. We had about eight dollars, enough for a tank of gas, a carton of cigarettes, and a couple of bags of chips.

We were sitting so far back from the stage that it looked like a speck, but at least I was sitting right by Jeremiah.

Jeremiah said, "You're cool, girl," and I almost levitated on that huge praise.

The exact second that Van Morrison took the stage, my left eye started to itch, so I scratched it. I swatted my arms, killing a family of mosquitoes and feeling the raised track of bites that went all the way down my arm. My right eye itched. My chest was burning. So was my neck. I started scratching everything, swatting mosquitoes, and feeling like I was crawling with ants.

I was. I was sitting on a tiny ant bed, and also seemed to be inside a private bubble of killer mosquitoes. I jumped up, stamping my feet. Jeremiah and his friends looked unaffected, and didn't register my alarm.

Jeremiah glanced at me and said, "What's with you? Oh, no."

I paused from my stamping and scratching and felt my face. I couldn't really, because it felt like my face was behind an inch of stretched-out putty, and my eyes were receding. My face was swelling like mad.

A girl standing next to me said, "You're in trouble, sister."

I thought so, too, and asked Jeremiah to go with me to get some kind of help.

"You'll be okay," he said, standing beside me. "Ride it out."

I said I had to drive somewhere to get ointment or something, and asked him to go with me.

"Be cool," he said. "You go on. We'll be fine."

He probably would be, since he and the nice girl next to me were splitting a beer.

I pushed my way through the throng, asked a guard for instructions to the drugstore, and got in my van. I got lost, and drove an hour before I found it.

The antihistamine started to work almost immediately, and I slathered calamine lotion all over my face, arms, and chest. Even with my swollen face and the pink on my arms, face, and neck, I was going back to the concert and sitting next to Jeremiah if it was the last thing I did.

I didn't, of course. On the way back to the concert, I ran out of gas and had to hitchhike back to the town where I got my ointment to buy some.

I swore that would be my last outdoor concert.

—Karla, 39, software designer, Boston

✳   ✳   ✳

Personal ads were my latest get-going step in dating. Instead of waiting for a guy to show up at my door one day wearing a name tag that read "YOUR FUTURE HUSBAND," I decided to follow the advice of those I-did-it-and-so-can-you books. However, I'd test the waters by answering an ad, not running one.

I responded to the one that read, "Professional, single black male, 5'11", 175 lbs. Works out daily. Handsome, churchgoing, loves music, theater, movies, cooking, traveling. Volunteer work. Devoted to golden retriever puppy. Send photo." I liked three things about that ad. First, he covered all the bases in a few lines. Second, he was a complete package. Third, I loved dogs but my landlady wouldn't let me have one.

A week after I sent him my photo and some details, he called, sounding friendly and sexy. His name was Harry.

"Let me prove that the ad doesn't lie," Harry said. "Come over and I'll cook you dinner. There'll be other people there. Come over Thursday night around seven-thirty. And you can meet my puppy."

How could I resist? He said his ad wouldn't lie, so how could it? My best friend said, "Here's what you would tell me in the same situation. You'd say, 'Don't get your hopes up. The guy could be the worst date you've ever had, and you'll be very disappointed. Anyone can write anything in those ads.' Just be casual. Don't pin too much on this guy."

I said, "Thanks a million for the pep talk."

I told myself that I wasn't being overly optimistic, I was being realistic. And at least I wasn't being my usual pessimistic self—like my friend was—about dating. I was going to be upbeat, upbeat, upbeat. I looked at my reflection in the bathroom mirror and got rid of the crease on my brow by saying, "Go, girl! Go!" until I believed myself.

I got to his house, rang the bell, and the most gorgeous guy I've ever seen, in skimpy running shorts, answered.

"Harry?" I asked, breathless with good fortune.

"No," said the hunk, "I'm his roommate. Come in."

In the living room, another hunk appeared, and I said, "Hi, Harry," and held out my hand.

He shook it, looked at me with obvious approval, and said, "I'm not Harry, but I wish I were. I'll go get him."

In pranced two more dreams—one man more gorgeous than the next—in chic suits, laughing, waving, and looking like a Christmastime whiskey ad as they left the house.

"You forgot your gloves!" shouted a man. He was about 5'3" and weighed about 175. He wasn't wearing a shirt, so his paunch flapped over the elastic waistband of his jogging shorts. His glasses had slipped down his nose and were barely hanging on. What hair he had left, it was clear even from a distance, he'd filled in with one of those products that sprays color onto your scalp.

I gasped before I could contain myself.

He turned to me and said, "Hi! I'm Harry! Sorry for the delay, but my roommates are going to a party, and they always need a little help getting ready."

Really? Looked to me like Harry had a little trouble getting ready. The roommates didn't need anything except me, I decided.

I didn't know what to say except "Help!" so I just stood there and plastered a smile on my face.

"Where's the puppy?" I asked, hoping for something pleasurable to focus on.

"The what? Oh!" He let out a heh-heh-heh, contorted laugh. "You liked that! The guys said babes would go for that. Heh-heh-heh. Let's go to the kitchen."

The skimpy splattering of chest hair was making my stomach turn.

"How about wearing a shirt while you cook?" I asked.

"Nah. Don't need one," he said. "A cooking impresario like myself needs lots of freedom," and he tried to give me a playful, debonair look that came off as stupid.

He rattled off the menu: ham, baked potatoes, and ice cream.

I stared hard at him and said, "Wow. You're really a gourmand, aren't you? Just one thing. I have to be home by nine-thirty, so let's get started. How can I help?"

His face fell, and instead of looking sad, he looked a little mean and said, "You're the third woman to answer my ad who's had to suddenly be home early. But I'm a good sport. You can check the ham. It's in the oven."

I wanted to say, "Why do you think the women freak? They expect Denzel Washington and instead they get . . . *you*."

I opened the oven, and didn't feel any heat.

"Is this on?" I asked, noticing that it wasn't. I peered inside the oven. Sitting on a rack was a can of ham. I took it out and put it on a counter. Yes, it was a cold, unopened can of ham.

He was taking two potatoes out of the microwave, and I decided to make sure I got out of his house fast.

"The ham's ready!" I said, cheerfully. I found a can opener and opened the can, scooping aside the congealed fat and cutting two hunks of ham, one for each of us. "You really are a fancy cook! Cold ham is all the rage these days!"

I waited for him to say, "Who do you think you're kidding? It needs heating," but he said, "Thanks. I know that."

He sat at the table without a shirt, too. The ham was cold, and the potatoes were hard as rocks. He put a carton of ice cream and two spoons on the table and said, "Dig in."

I pushed around the entree, then moved directly to dessert. I pried loose a small chunk of rock-solid ice cream. I didn't want to put it beside my ham, so I quickly ate it off my spoon and got an ice cream headache that made me reel. I took my plate, glass of water, and utensils to the sink, and said, "Thanks for dinner! Gotta run!"

Before I could leave the kitchen, he said, "Tell it to me straight. What turns you off? I need to know."

Normally, I would have said, "Nothing. Not a thing. Really. It's just that we aren't a good match, and one day you'll find someone who appreciates you for who you are . . ."

This time, I said, "You should wear a shirt and shoes when you cook for a date. You should order takeout food. You shouldn't lie in your ads. You shouldn't be living with men who look like male models, and you certainly should never, ever, in a million years, have lied about the puppy. That hurt," and I left.

—Lee, 23, writer, Seattle

* * *

"Positive," I told my college roommate. "I'm positive that we have a date tonight. It's definite."

I'd come home to my dorm room this morning on cloud nine. I had spent the night with a guy, André, whom I was crazy about.

He was a junior, from France, and we'd been making eyes at each other for months when we'd see each other at a pub near campus.

Last night, Friday night, André and I had walked into the pub at the same time, bumping shoulders as we entered, and we'd starting talking. He had a devastating smile, sandy blond hair, long legs, and a great way of lifting one eyebrow when he was making fun of himself. He sat with me and my friends, but he and I spent the whole time talking, even after my friends left.

He said he'd walk me home, and we wound up going to his dorm room, where I spent the night, waking to find that I was smitten.

I told my roommate about André's parting words: "I'll see you at the pub tonight."

I told my roommate, "That means we have a date tonight. How could we *not* after last night?"

My roommate said, "Sounds like you're trying to talk yourself into believing you have a date, which means you don't. You're too smart a girl for that."

I looked at her in horror. Hadn't she been listening? Was she brain-dead? I glared at her and replied, "What you're forgetting is that last night constitutes a full-fledged date. We spent the night together, so now we're dating. . . . Except, maybe he said, 'I'll *probably* see you at the pub tonight.' No, I'm positive we have a date tonight. We're *dating*."

My roommate stared at me a little more and said, "Bad news. He plays around."

I almost keeled over, but collected myself, lifted my head, and said, "So what? We're not getting married. But I'm positive we have a date tonight. He's not the kind of guy who'd take last night lightly."

My roommate grimaced and turned away. For a few seconds I realized what an idiot I was being, then I decided to examine the facts from my newly contorted point of view, and concluded that I certainly did have a date.

That night, André never showed up at the pub. My roommate shot me "told-you-so" looks, and I was starting to believe her—and my common sense. At eleven o'clock, I announced, "He's probably waiting for me at his dorm. I'll see you later."

Once I was on his floor, I waved at his next-door neighbor, who was leaving. The neighbor had an odd expression on his face, but I was on a mission and didn't have the time or interest to find out what that was about.

I knocked at André's door.

No answer. I thought I heard a noise, so I knocked again, certain someone was home. I knocked harder, and kept knocking, until two doors down the hall opened and male heads poked out to stare at me. It was a small dorm, on a small campus, so I recognized them from my English class.

I stared back, embarrassed, then, while they continued to watch me, knocked again. I couldn't turn back now. I'd been seen, so I couldn't have escaped unnoticed if I'd wanted to.

Might as well finish the job.

I grabbed his doorknob and slowly turned it. I gingerly pushed the door open halfway, noticing that the room was dark. He wasn't home—he was waiting for me at the pub. I smiled, relieved, and started to close the door.

"Yeah, who is there?" It was André's voice, coming from the middle of the room. That's when the lightbulb went on in my head—and stayed on.

I heard the unmistakeable sounds of people repositioning themselves in bed, and heard a female sigh. I started blushing so hard that I was perspiring. That was pure humiliation.

All I could say, still grasping the doorknob, was, "Hi. Well, I'll see you later!"

I yanked the door closed, and stood in the hall with the back of my head against the door.

It was clear that what we'd had last night was completely meaningless to him. And it was clear that everyone on the floor, particularly the guys who were still standing in their doorways watching, would know what a fool I'd been.

At that moment, everything became so clear. There had never been a date. What kind of thinking had led me to this? Why hadn't my roommate been more of a help in decoding this situation?

I was so embarrassed, I couldn't have gone anywhere with André again—even if he *had* called.

—Eileen, 21, student, New Jersey

✳ ✳ ✳

My friend and I were hanging out at our local bar and dance club. The bartender, whom I'd gone to high school with, said, "Are you dating anyone steady? . . . Then I've got this nice guy I want you to meet. You game?"

The bartender had just met the guy, and there were several reasons why I would ordinarily have passed. For instance, what a guy thought was a good dating prospect for a woman was always bad news—they had no idea what type of date a woman wants. Second, why would I assume that the bartender could get a good fix on a new patron he'd exchanged two sentences with over blasting music?

With those smart, clearheaded reasons to pass on the offer, I said, "Sure, I'll meet him."

I didn't want to make an issue out of something as simple as an introduction. I hadn't met anyone new in a long time, and the guy would probably be a zero; after a few minutes, I'd blow him off and be back where I started from, nothing gained, nothing lost. Having talked myself into defying logic, I let the bartender wave him over.

Imagine my surprise to be looking into Kevin Costner's face. The guy's medium-length straight black hair occasionally fell over one eye, and he gave me a movie-star grin. It only took one glance for me to see, as he got to his feet, that he was tall and in great shape. The bartender was grinning like a hyena and yelled, "Told you so!"

His name was Brant, and he bought me and my girlfriend beers. He danced with me three times, and once with my friend, which I thought was nice. He was a painter and had started teaching art at a community center. He had moved to town to be near his parents, though he had been living upstate. When he asked me for my phone number, I didn't hesitate.

We had a lunch date at a pizzeria, and he was charming. I was lucking out. At the end of lunch, he said, "If you want to see me again, you'll have to meet my parole officer."

The red-and-white-checked tablecloth started to swim, then I said, "Very funny. You got me for a second there."

He looked serious and said, "This isn't a joke, What did you think I meant when I said I'd been living upstate? I was in Sing Sing Correctional Facility in Ossining. Do you know what I mean?"

How would I know what he meant? I had assumed he had a cute cottage in the country, not a cell in a prison.

I choked out, "Do you mind if I ask what you were in for?"

He didn't blink an eye. "I'd think you were a fool if you didn't," he said casually. "Ten counts of armed robbery."

I gasped, put a hand on my purse where I had two hundred dollars in cash, and scanned the place for the exit.

Brant said, "Don't get excited! I thought you could handle this! Relax! Relax! Put your purse down. Listen, I'm not violent. I just didn't want to steal money from my parents for my drug habit, and I thought it was logical to steal from other people. You can see that, can't you? Not that what I did is right, right?"

I listened, gave him a hard once-over, and said, "Sure. If

you think I'm that gullible, you don't know me very well. Cute story. So, when do we move on to a dinner date?"

He'd broken into a big grin, shook his head, and said, "Saturday night a good enough dinner date for you?"

The next day I thought about calling to cancel. I still thought he had been pulling my leg. But what if he had been telling the truth? Only a fool would go out with a guy who said he had a parole officer for a chaperone, right? And even if that weren't so bad, wouldn't only a fool go out with a guy like that to whom she had no connection, no mutual friend of any kind?

However, he had two things in his favor: He was great-looking and sincere.

Saturday night, on the way to dinner, he said he had to stop by his parents' house first.

They were nice—reminded me of my own parents.

Brant said, "Pa, tell her. She thinks it's a joke."

"Ah, no, it's no joke," said his dad as if he were discussing picking up the wrong hat from a rack. "It was armed robbery all right. Bunch of times. But he's a new man now. Have you seen any of his artwork yet? You should see this. He started painting at Ossining."

He sure did. I wanted to load up a gun when I saw the paintings in the living room. One was more violent than the next—renditions of blood spurting from the chest of a man hurtling backward, of a spray of bullets coming out of a car window, and on and on.

His mother said, "They say he has talent. He was even teaching a class to the other inmates, he was so good."

Not that dinner wasn't good, but he didn't have much to say, having been tucked away at Sing Sing for so long. Also, on the ride home, while he was telling me I had to meet his parole officer, he said, "You like cocaine? Want to go with me to score some? Why not?"

I said that I didn't do drugs, never dated anyone who did, and could tell that we weren't a good match.

He insisted that we were. He called me for a couple of

weeks, but I let my answering machine pick up his calls and had my secretary screen him out.

Usually I didn't meet my date's parents so soon, and I certainly never followed up the meet-the-parents with meet-the-parole-officer, and I surely didn't want to get involved with a guy doing drugs—especially one who already had a prison record.

When I told all this to the bartender I had gone to school with, he said, "Bummer. So you're not going out with him again?"

—Madeline, 25, marketing, New York

❋ ❋ ❋

Boredom made me reckless. I felt especially impulsive in Japan.

I was twenty-two, and disenchanted with traditional careers, and had wanted to live abroad. Being an English teacher in Japan was an instant way to add spice to my life.

Except I didn't have a love life.

Every morning when I stood on the subway platform on my way to work, I'd see the same gorgeous man seated calmly reading a newspaper, and my fantasy world would kick in. He would be Italian, a famous soccer player, and we would be destined to be together.

After three months of sneaking peeks at him, one day, against my better judgment, I took action. I scribbled my name and phone number on a piece of paper and waited. I always got off the train before he did. My plan was to hand him the paper as I disembarked. I'd never given a complete stranger my number before and I knew it was chancy, but I wasn't even sure if anything would come of it.

I stood by the doors, and as they opened, I handed him the paper. He smiled, and I stepped off.

All day at work, I was thrilled. I had finally added some intrigue to my life in Japan! I told everyone about what I'd done, and they were surprised, too.

My boss looked me square in the eyes and said, "Don't ever do that again. It's dangerous, and at best it could be awful."

She had a point, but I was young, carefree—and I knew better than to do what I had done. Back in the States, I would never have done anything so ridiculous or risky.

When he hadn't called by the end of the day, I was grateful for at least providing myself with an interesting conversation piece. And I was grateful that my stupid action hadn't progressed into anything more than a note. The guy was obviously brighter and more sensible than I was.

As I was leaving, my phone rang and a sexy, heavily accented voice asked for me. It was him!

José was from Spain, loved soccer, but was a businessman. My wish list was almost a match to the real thing! He said he'd noticed me all these months, too, and that I was beautiful.

That was when my knees shook and I had to sit down. This fantasy was coming alive. I had actually put some wheels in motion.

I accepted a date for Friday. He said he would orchestrate the entire evening. He wanted to meet me on the subway platform, "where our eyes first met," he said. I took a seat and waited. There he was, holding a red rose, wearing sexy cologne, looking beyond handsome.

I stood up, our eyes locked, and I realized that the trajectory was downward. This was the first time I had ever seen him on his feet instead of sitting down. I was at least four inches taller. That was the first glitch in my private movie.

On the train, he presented me with the rose, held my free hand, and put his other arm around my shoulders, and whispered, "*Que bella*, how beautiful you are," and I started giggling. I never giggle, but I couldn't stop. The situation was so absurd!

The Japanese, who never show emotion in public, were watching us intently.

He had chosen a Spanish restaurant where he was a regular. On his behalf, the owner had set up a private table just for us, right in the middle of the dance floor. It had two tall candles and a spotlight from the ceiling. It was too much. We'd be on display as lovers! I started giggling again.

He tried to feed me shrimp, and I said, "The last person who fed me was my mother, so I've outgrown this. I can feed myself," but he insisted, trying to pry open my gritted teeth with the tail of the shrimp, which made me laugh, providing him an opportunity to pop the shrimp into my mouth, whereupon I swallowed it whole. Looking serious, he came toward my mouth with another shrimp, and I started laughing again.

He told me all about himself and didn't ask much about me. His first and last names were José. He was José José, which made me lean over sideways, I was laughing so hard.

Then he told me a fact that sobered me up fast. He was eighteen.

I said, "Pardon me? You're a teenager?"

The night was not over. He took me to a disco where the deejay played the very worst disco songs ever recorded, and José José began to gyrate his hips in big motions all over the place, punching the air over his head, which made me laugh again.

At our table, he said, "I have something for you. It's in my pants. Reach into my pocket and take it."

I laughed harder and said, "I bet you do!" and I slapped the table, it was so funny. This was the weirdest, goofiest date I'd ever been on.

He said, "Please. There's something in here that I think you'll be happy about."

My stomach hurt so much that I tried not to laugh at all and I gasped, "Would any other man in here have one of these?"

He pulled back and said, "What? What do you take me for? That is crass. No! It is a gift."

Feeling foolish, I reached in and pulled a plastic bag, praying that a prophylactic wasn't inside. Too bad there wasn't.

It was a necklace: a charm of a very high-heeled shoe, with my first name monogrammed on the back.

A stiletto-heel necklace? I definitely didn't have one of these already. He put it around my neck, saying, "I'll buy all your jewelry from now on," and started kissing my neck and my earlobes, which tickled so much that I started laughing again.

He looked at me with surprise, not understanding why I thought this was funny, and I saw that he had one of my clip-on hoop earrings in his mouth, and laughed even harder.

I pointed to his mouth. He felt his lips and put the hoop on the table.

I said, "I have to go home. My stomach hurts very badly."

He took me to my bus, and I sat by the window. All of a sudden I heard singing in a male voice, and looked out my window. There was my date, down on one knee, serenading me with love songs. I started laughing, and everyone on the bus stood to look at José José and at me.

As the bus pulled away, he yelled, his hands over his heart, "Love is beautiful!" which made me bend over and laugh.

He called me every day, five times a day, for a week, never taking my gentle hints or, eventually, my direct refusals.

He was too much for me. And too young for me. I alternated between feeling bad—after all, I was the one who got this thing started—and feeling annoyed—after all, he was completely over the top. He thought we were starting a whirlwind, passionate romance; I thought it was the silliest date I'd ever been on, and it was the result of one of the dumbest impulses I'd ever acted on. When I was getting in the happy habit of complaining about his love for me, he stopped calling. I missed those calls.

Now, when I'm bored and my wheels start turning, I remember José José in Japan, and I repeat one important rule for living and dating: There is never, ever, anything better than a proper introduction, particularly when you're feeling reckless.

—Jill, 24, English teacher, New Orleans

✳ ✳ ✳

Why was there a ring of waiters standing in front of us smiling—at me? My boyfriend Emmett was spooning chocolate mousse into his mouth, and he was looking at me, too. What was the attraction? Had my blouse fallen off or something?

A few hours earlier, Emmett had called me at work. It was December 23, one of the busiest days of the year for me. It was also his birthday. He was also leaving for New Zealand the next day to visit his family for three weeks.

"Tonight, you can take me out for a drink," he said. "Then you can take me to the steak house for a big dinner. That'll be my birthday and Christmas gift. That's all I want! I want to spend my last night doing something romantic with you."

I said, "I don't think so. I'm bushed. The customers are coming in like we're the only store in town. I couldn't even take a break today. I was thinking we'd have pizza or something at home, and celebrate for real when you got back."

I had a roaring headache, my feet were killing me, and besides, I told him, "I'm grumpy, and I'm sleepy. I don't want to go out. I'm no fun."

He said, "Oh, come on. Tonight is my *birthday*. This is a simple present. And I'm leaving tomorrow for almost a month. Come on."

I said, "No. No, no, no. I'm exhausted. I just want to go home and get into my robe and then crawl into bed. No way."

Emmett said, "Great. I'll spend my birthday by myself."

I said, "I'm not going out tonight. We can have pizza at

home, and I'll take you out for a big dinner when you get back. I promise. But I know that I won't be good company tonight, and I'm certain that I'm too tired to sit through dinner. I'll just insist on going home the minute we get seated. This is one of those times when I have to put my own needs first and not feel guilty about it. I need to go home and sleep. No, no, no."

So that's how I wound up seated beside him at the steak house. At least we had comfortable seats. We'd lucked into a semicircular upholstered booth.

We had a glass of wine, and I told my date, "I'm too tired to look at a menu. You order for me."

He did. He ordered shrimp appetizers, salads, huge steaks, baked potatoes with a side order of fries just for him, garlic bread, and a bottle of wine.

"That's going to take a long time to eat," I said. "I want to go home. I'm tired."

He poured me a fresh glass of wine and said, "Be a sport. Once you eat something, you'll feel better."

That was just a few seconds ago, wasn't it?

So what was with the waiters? I scratched my neck and found a big cloth napkin tucked into my collar.

"What's going on?" I asked.

My boyfriend scooped more mousse into his mouth and said, "You fell asleep, that's what. Before the appetizers even. And I thought you'd wake up, but you didn't, so I leaned your head back against the booth, because you were nodding forward, and I tucked that napkin in your collar because you were drooling a little. Just a little bit."

I rubbed the crick in my neck and said, "So you ate a complete meal while I took a nap?"

One of the waiters said, "Nap?"

"That wasn't a nap," said my boyfriend, "that was a good sleep. You snored a couple of times."

"NO!" I cried, wanting to slide under the table. I noticed that people at nearby tables were looking at me and smiling.

I must have been a pretty sight with my head back, sound asleep, a napkin on my chest, my mouth open, snoring, while my date ate away. Worse yet, the waiters were still grinning at me.

"Why are the waiters here?" I asked, trying not to look too embarrassed.

"Oh. I woke you up because they're ready to serve me my slice of birthday cake with the candle, and they were hoping you'd wake up for it so they wouldn't scare you when they started singing. Ready?"

I was speechless. I shrugged, they sang, he blew out the candle, and I said, "I told you I was too tired. I told you so. Why didn't I listen to myself? Now ask them to wrap up that cake and put it in a doggie bag, because I'm out of here."

I took the candle out of the cake, pushed the plate toward a waiter, and had to listen to my date actually say, "That was the best birthday dinner I ever had. It was brilliant. Thank you," and he kissed me on the cheek just as my stomach growled.

—Josephine, 29, manager, department store, Midland, Texas

❋   ❋   ❋

10

✳ ✳ ✳ ✳

When It Works

Dating requires so much effort and too much hopefulness, right? Retiring your dating spurs sounds like a good idea. It's so much easier to stay home with a video or hang with friends. Even so, tonight you'll rally and go out on *one more date*. And guess what? This time, after some rough going, it's actually smooth sailing. It works out, just like it's supposed to. And romance, finally, is right in front of you, and it's yours.

Strategy, strategy, that's what my longtime buddy George was saying into the phone when he called me at my office. I was declining his offer to go out for a drink.

"The strategy is to keep dating, to keep looking for chicks," George informed me. "You're working too hard. You've got to go out. Is this about Erica? Are you moping or something? Get over it. Forget about her. That was months ago."

Maybe it was months ago, but I had come close to proposing marriage on the same afternoon that she had announced that she was leaving the country with a guy I'd introduced her to at a party. I hadn't had enough time to get over it. And I didn't want to go out for a drink. I wanted to go home and feed my parakeet and watch Mary Tyler Moore reruns.

"Remember our game plan when we were kids? We could dust off that old routine. How about it?"

I distinctly remembered that the strategy of casually bumping into girls we'd been following had never worked out for us.

I gave in, but with restrictions: "Let's just go to a neighborhood bar. One drink. I don't want to go a club. No trying to pick up anyone. Got it?"

We stepped into an Upper West Side bar and restaurant called Palsson's. At the elbow of the L-shaped bar were two girls. I looked around. They were the only ones in the place besides us.

I headed for a table in the back, but George grabbed my arm and steered me right toward the two women. He took a bar stool next to one of them, and I slid onto a stool next to him. We formed a perfect L.

The girl on the far end looked excited and said, "Here! Have some fish crackers! They're great."

The girl sitting next to George rolled her eyes and looked around.

George didn't care. He was interested in the girl who was interested, and he started jabbering, ordering drinks for all of us. He and the girl, Pam, were talking nonstop.

I stole a glance at the bored girl. She was cute, but bent out of shape. She hadn't counted on a babehound like George to sit right next to them in an otherwise deserted bar. I got a kick out of this, and was glad I didn't have to do any talking.

The place got crowded, and the bar area filled to capacity.

The quiet girl, Holly, looked around at the crowd and got up to play the jukebox. George immediately slid onto her stool, pulling me with him so that I had to sit where he'd been sitting. When Holly came back, she couldn't believe that her seat was taken and that she'd been moved to the end of our line. She sat on my vacated stool and, cross, said to me, "I just got relocated."

I waited for something witty to come out of my mouth, but I hung my head and mumbled, "Yeah."

She stared at me, then turned to her left, where a guy had taken the last free bar stool and was reading a book of poetry. She said, "How can you read in here with all this noise?" and he swiveled away from her. I knew I should have tried to rescue her, but I was tongue-tied. I could have killed myself.

She was making the best of it, and I had turned to stone. After spending the last eight years of my life studying like a maniac, I had forgotten my social skills. I was rusty.

A guy asked her to dance and she did, and suddenly George's interest turned from Pam to Holly. That made me come alive. When Holly sat back down, I asked what she did, where she was from, and how old she was, and stored the information. She was from San Antonio, was twenty-four, worked at a music magazine. She asked what I did. I didn't want to ruin things by being boring, so I said, "I'm a drummer in a Rastafarian band."

I smiled when her eyes got big and she checked out my penny loafers, blazer, button-down shirt, and khakis. "That's great," she said sincerely, then danced with another guy.

When she danced with him a second time, I noticed that he was the hipster in a leather jacket who had introduced himself as Angel. He'd told her that he worked at a nightclub when he wasn't modeling.

Angel looked a little ratty to me, and I was nervous about him dancing with Holly. I was feeling protective and decided to rescue her.

As the song ended, I swiveled on my bar stool, got to my feet, and said, "The next dance is mine."

The music stopped, and Angel and Holly looked at me. I cleared my voice and took Holly's hand, and we started to dance to a slow tune.

Testing me, Holly asked, "What songs does your band play?"

I said, "Mostly Marley."

Angel glared from the sidelines. When the song was over,

I steered her to the far end of the dance floor and made sure we were inaccessible.

When we sat down again, I put my arm behind her, grasping the bottom of her stool, and gave Angel what I hoped was my best get-lost stare.

George was saying, "Hey, Holly! How long have you and Pam been friends?"

But Holly hopped up to dance with Angel again, and I wanted to slam a glass onto my forehead.

I liked this girl, had come by her honestly—no strategies at all—and she kept slipping away. I liked her short brown hair. I liked her brown eyes. And I liked the way she looked when she talked. But I didn't even know her last name. George, on the other hand, already had Pam's phone number and was arranging a Friday night date. Even the poet was coming alive, looking interested in Holly, but he'd had his chance.

Holly danced with Angel two more times and said she'd probably meet him there Friday night with some of her friends who also liked to dance. I wanted to tell her not to do it.

She and I talked a little more, then it was time to go. George asked for her number, saying he'd call her because he was arranging a party. I held my breath. I was sure that Pam held hers. But Holly laughed and shook her head, and George seemed to like that, nodding and smiling at me, as if he were telling me that she'd passed a test.

The four of us left together. Pam and George were both getting cabs, and Holly said she was walking home. Ever the gallant gentleman that I was, I asked if I could walk her home.

The first few blocks, we didn't say much. I couldn't figure out what to say to break the ice, so I started whistling, and I took her hand and linked it under my elbow. She smiled and said, "That's nice," and, magically, we started talking.

In front of her apartment building, I asked for her phone number, and she thought for a second, then handed me a business card and smiled.

I pulled her into a kiss, then stepped back and hailed a cab.

I called her for a Friday night date, intentionally trying to eclipse Angel, and succeeded. I told her we would go dancing at the Ritz, to hear Robin Leach and the Chart Busters. She said, "You mean Robin Lane? Or Tom Petty and the Heartbreakers? You're a drummer, right?"

That night, over dinner at my favorite Greek restaurant, I told her I was an intern at a hospital, and she laughed, asking if she could still introduce me to her friends as a Rastafarian drummer.

On our third date, she told me she had thought I was cute and sweet when I'd been in Palsson's, but was shy, and that she'd been hoping I'd talk to her more. She thought I had been giving her a brush-off.

At the end of our fourth date, I told her that I was falling hard, and she confessed that she had already fallen a little bit when I walked her home that first night and kissed her. She'd had a flash of insight that we'd be having a relationship.

That was years ago. Now we've been married seven years. George, who rightly takes credit for getting me and Holly together, was in our wedding.

Holly and I just took an apartment in her old neighborhood. The first night that we moved in, we walked to a restaurant, and on the way back, I kissed her. She pointed to a street lamp and said, "That's the same spot where you gave me our first kiss."

And it was, so she kissed me again.

—Will, 35, doctor, New York City

* * *